A TIME TO LAUGH

Smyth & Helwys Publishing, Inc.
6316 Peake Road
Macon, Georgia 31210-3960
1-800-747-3016
©2013 by Mark E. Biddle
All rights reserved.
Printed in the United States of America.

ISBN 978-1-57312-683-0

Library of Congress Control Number: 2013940980

A Time *to* Laugh

HUMOR IN THE BIBLE

MARK E. BIDDLE

Also by Mark Biddle

A Redaction History of Jeremiah 2:1-4:2

Polyphony and Symphony in Prophetic Literature: A Literary Analysis of Jeremiah 7–20 (Studies in Old Testament Interpretation)

Deuteronomy (Smyth & Helwys Bible Commentary)

Missing the Mark: Sin and Its Consequences in Biblical Theology

Judges (Reading the Old Testament)

To my wife Priscilla
because she knows that
"Laughter is the shortest distance between two people." (Victor Borge)

Contents

Introduction

"No man who has once heartily and wholly laughed can be altogether irreclaimably bad." (Thomas Carlyle)

As an introduction to the topic of humor in the Bible, it will be helpful, perhaps even essential, to set the subject in some context. I want to be clear from the beginning that I am not interested in (and have no reason to be interested in) *making* the Bible funny. Nor am I interested in religious jokes. People sometimes enroll in the seminary course I teach or attend church presentations I give on the subject, thinking that I am going to supply them with a treasury of the jokes preachers need to begin a sermon or to throw into the mix midway should the congregation's attention wander. I could do that, I suppose, but it is not the focus of my interest in Bible humor.

Instead, the focus of my interest derives from the realization that came to me some years ago that there is actually humor in the Bible. At points, in other words, the Bible is actually *funny*—and intentionally so. Teaching undergraduates early in my career typically involved nine sections in the course of an academic year and perhaps extra sections in summer terms. Since Religion 101, "Introduction to the Old Testament," was a general education requirement, my job involved teaching Old Testament seven or eight times a year, plus any summer teaching I did because the institution needed the offering and, as a young professor, I needed the extra pay. So, in ten years of undergraduate teaching, I taught the introduction course at least eighty times to well over 2,500 students. Needless to say, by the end of my tenure teaching at the undergraduate level, I could teach Old Testament without relying on my notes.

Once, toward the end of that ten years, I was lecturing to a class of honors freshmen, probably for the seventy-ninth iteration, doing my theological exposition in the properly professorial and serious manner, when something in the biblical text I was discussing suddenly and unexpectedly struck me as funny. I actually chuckled to myself. More than that, because I was not sure that it would have been appropriate in the setting, I had to stifle a good laugh, resisting the urge to stop and let myself fully experience the humor I had just recognized. This was a new experience for me. I had taught this text probably seventy-eight times before and had never heard any humor in it. I made a mental note to myself that when class was over, back in my office, I would consider the phenomenon, and I dutifully continued the lecture.

In the office later, three possibilities seemed likely to me. One possibility was that I had become punch-drunk, that over-familiarity with the text—I was, I am ashamed to admit, functioning somewhat on autopilot, after all—had caused me to see myself as a comic figure, which I regularly do. I amuse myself more than may be suitable for a pious minister and serious Bible scholar. The second possibility was that I was having a cross-cultural experience, that the biblical author was simply narrating events that, from his perspective, were absolutely matter-of-fact and humorless but that, from my perspective as a then-twentieth-century east Tennessean, second-millennium ancient Near Eastern behavior was odd, and I had found it funny. The third possibility, unheard of to me at the time, was that the biblical author meant this text to be humorous. Could it be that this was indeed a truly funny story? Is there authentic, intentional comedy in the Bible?

It seemed that I needed more information and more time to think about this question. I did what I always do in these cases. I have a drawer where I keep file folders with notes on potential research topics—ideas I might one day investigate further in order to teach a course or write an article or a book. I started a file on humor in the Bible. Over time, I added notes on readings I came across, on additional texts in the Bible that seemed to contain humor, on questions to resolve were I ever to deal with the topic seriously and comprehensively, and so forth. I came to teach at the seminary some years later, and my turn to represent the Bible area in the January term course rolled around. As it happens, I dislike mini-term courses. What can one cover adequately in three weeks? How do students and professors alike maintain energy and focus in such intensive contexts? In a curriculum-planning meeting, the dean turned to me and asked me to propose a course. Musing aloud more than making a serious proposal, I commented that I had been interested for some time in the possibility of exploring humor in the Bible. "Humor in the Bible, it is," he said, "Monday through Friday, 9 AM to 12 noon, room 121," and I was committed. Well, I thought, I doubt that there is enough material in my file folder to constitute a whole fifteen-lecture, forty-five-contact-hour course. Obviously, I was going to have to research the topic and give it careful thought. As it turned out, I prepared the course with enough material and to spare. I now teach it in regular semesters on a rotating basis. Students seem to find it enlightening and useful.

A Basic Definition: The Recognition of Incongruity

My discoveries in the library were quite eye opening. Above all, I discovered that humor and the comic are serious topics of study in several disciplines. Psychologists are very interested in the subject, as are sociologists, anthropologists, philosophers, and political scientists—in short, anyone who is interested in some aspect of what it means to be a human being and in how human beings behave, think, and feel. In fact, a long discussion tracing back at least to Aristotle deals with what humor is, how it functions, what defines a "sense of humor," the significance of the fact that humans have such a sense, and how it may vary with culture, gender, class, status, and so forth. The discussion is fascinating, although sometimes surprisingly complex. In the seminary course, we spend a couple of weeks on this complicated contextual material. For the purposes of this book, however, I can summarize that discussion in terms of a few pivotal insights that provide key terms and concepts for what will follow. We all have unique senses of humor; we all know what we think is funny. In order to talk about a commonly held understanding and to deal with an ancient literature, which comes to us from cultures not our own and in three foreign, dead languages (biblical Hebrew, Aramaic, and *koine* Greek), however, it is important to have a working definition. That is, if, when looking for humor in the Bible, we must make a leap across time, space, customs, and language, we need a clear idea about what we seek. Otherwise, we may not recognize it even when it would have been obvious to the ancient Israelites or the early Christians.

The consensus definition in the scholarly literature is that the sense of humor, the experience of the comic, involves the recognition of incongruity. To illustrate this concept, I often tell a story that dates back a few years to a period when all of my children (boy, boy, girl, boy) were still at home. I am not a Luddite; I am not afraid of technology. On the other hand, I do not want to become enslaved to it or to the impulse to keep abreast of the most recent trend. Thus, I often resist new gadgets—at least for a while. For a few years, I resisted cell phones, for example. Nonetheless, they have turned out to be gifts from God. I am sure that my wife and I could have survived without them, but our lives would have been very different and certainly much more complicated.

By the time our children were in middle school, they were heavily involved in music. In addition to regular school, work, and church activities, it seemed that every night someone had a lesson, a rehearsal, or a concert, and, not infrequently, two or more of the children would be involved in different activities. Meanwhile, I would have speaking engagements or seminary events to attend, and my wife, who is also a teacher, would have parent-night meetings and the like on her calendar. It was not at all unusual, say on a Tuesday or Wednesday afternoon, for my wife to call me on the cell phone to say, "You know what? I just remembered that one of the children has to be driven to a rehearsal at 6:30, and you have a speaking engagement an hour away. So you'll be leaving before 6:00. And I have a called faculty meeting after school today, so I won't be able to get home before 5:30. What are we going to do about dinner? I left out some hamburger meat to thaw this morning."

Incidentally, I was usually intelligent enough to recognize the last statement as a hint. Thus, the problem-resolution phase of our day began.

I am an excellent *sous-chef.* Typically, I would prep and start dinner, then grab a sandwich and hand off the spatula to my wife when she walked in the door so I could depart for my appointment. In cases like this, when I did not want or have time to change clothes, I would remove my suit coat, of course, and don the only apron we had that was large enough to meet the need, a bibbed Christmas apron, green and red, with a depiction of a headless Santa Claus. The cook supplies Santa's head. My teenaged children simply loved to come home from school and find me in the kitchen in business suit and Santa Claus apron regardless of the season. I wore it because it fit, not because I was trying to enhance the ambience of the kitchen or perpetuate a seasonal theme, and principally because I wanted to keep grease off my tie. The children, however, thought it was the most hilarious thing they had ever seen.

Why? What took place in those moments? The children recognized the incongruity inherent in the circumstance. How many different roles was I fulfilling in those moments? Outwardly, I was impersonating Santa Claus in June. Functionally, I was the modern husband doing my part in the kitchen, goofily, to be sure, but doing it nonetheless. Peeling away the silly apron, I was the seminary professor, holder of an endowed chair, still dressed in my professional attire in anticipation of lecturing or preaching later that evening. All the while, of course, I was Dad—the disciplinarian, the authority figure—a serious role indeed for someone dressed in a dark suit, tie, and Santa Claus apron. Incongruity in abundance!

Corollaries: Catharsis and the Uncontrollable Comic

Scholars in various disciplines agree on this basic definition of humor or the comic. They also share a general consensus on a number of corollaries. Students of humor agree, for example, that one of the common results of an experience of the comic, of the recognition of some incongruity, is a feeling of catharsis, a feeling of release. Human beings experience a sense of relief when the tension inherent in the incongruity is resolved by recognition. This experience of catharsis is an essential component of human sensibility. Even toddlers who have not yet acquired language, let alone the complicated system of social and cultural conventions necessary to comprehend more complex humor, display evidence of this experience of relief in games such as "peek-a-boo" and in their reactions to jack-in-the-box and similar toys. The mother who hides her face, often even while asking the question, "Where did she go? Where is Mama?" introduces tension. The infant reacts involuntarily to her reappearance, the resolution of the tension, with peals of laughter. "There she is!" She has not gone away permanently, as the child may instinctively fear. This reaction to the return of an absent loved one shapes the fundamental human capacities for hope, joy, and playfulness. It is inherent in the human sense of humor.

Further, since the context against which one recognizes an incongruity varies with a person's individual and cultural experience, researchers agree that the "sense of humor" is somewhat subjective and linked to one's culture. This is not to say that the phenomenon of humor is *entirely* subjective. One of the most defining characteristics of being human is the sense of humor. Babies in all cultures laugh well before they acquire language and all the cultural norms and expectations associated with it. Indeed, much like the distinction between the capacity for language and the acquisition of a specific language, a child's sense of humor is innate as a capacity. As the child grows, learns language, and becomes acculturated, the culture shapes the child's expectations of "normal" against which a humorous incongruity can be experienced, but the capacity for humor precedes this learning and acculturation.

Indeed, the sense of humor is so fundamental that it often resists the control that a society or even the individual experiencing the comic might try to exert on it. Humor scholars point to the *physical* or *autonomous* character of the comic; genuine laughter is an involuntary reflex. Humor involves an *ecstatic* component; it is experienced passively and is often uncontrollable. Often, too, humor is *intrusive*; it originates outside the person experiencing it. Together, these aspects of humor make the experience of the comic a potentially *subversive* factor in the lives of individuals and in society; as the recognition of incongruity, humor often points out that the emperor has no clothes.

In order to relate this rather analytical description of the human sense of humor to common experience, it is only necessary to remember some time in one's life when the absurdly comic character of an otherwise solemn moment became overwhelming, uncontrollable. The effort to stifle laughter—to maintain one's composure in social settings in which laughter seems inappropriate—often only makes matters worse. Who has not suddenly been struck by the incongruity of the words of a hymn, the attire of a great-aunt, or the behavior of a young cousin at a wedding or a funeral and fought the urge to laugh? Everyone has seen clips of television news reporters overcome by the humor of slips of the tongue on their part or the part of a colleague: the incongruity of a professional communicator who proves, in the end, to be a fallible human being. Often, in such circumstances, the more one tries to control oneself, the more uncontrollable one's laughter becomes. The truth will not be denied: humor involves the intrusive, sometimes disruptive, recognition of incongruity. As the saying goes, "You may as well laugh about it; otherwise, you would have to cry." In other words, although intrusive, such an acknowledgment of incongruity also releases one from the tension of denial, producing catharsis.

Implications for Reading the Bible

There are several implications of this basic definition and its corollaries. Obviously, an awareness of the comic dimension of existence, a sense of humor, characterizes human beings at a basic level and represents a powerful force in human psychology and sociology. Therefore, one of the questions that intrigues me has to do with the fact that I was well into my thirties, holding several advanced degrees in biblical studies and theology, a professor of religion, before I ever noticed any humor in the Bible. Humor may have long been a topic of discussion among anthropologists and philosophers, but students of the Bible have not even acknowledged that the Bible contains humor, at least not until recently. Admittedly, a few scholars have turned attention to humor in the Bible in the last ten or fifteen years, but for two centuries or more in the history of the modern study of Scripture, this was not the case. What might explain the silence?

First, a number of obstacles that confront modern readers hinder the recognition of incongruity in the Bible, the chief being the fact that we have the Bible in translation. Much of the humor in the Bible involves *paronomasia* or word play. One can imagine how difficult it is to translate the occasional pun in Hebrew into a serviceable corresponding pun in English. The attempt can be maddening. Scholars frequently surrender and simply add a footnote, "The Hebrew involves a pun on Isaac's name," or something similar. Readers of the translation may trust the translator that this is so, but they may not be able to "get" the humor based on such comments.

In addition to problems involved with translating the language, there are also problems related to translating cultures. Had Father Abraham been transported forward in time and brought into my kitchen on some occasion when, clad in Santa Claus apron, dress shirt, and tie, I was beginning dinner preparations, he would probably not have known that anything was out of the ordinary, incongruous. Everything about my behavior and appearance would likely have been foreign to him. He may have concluded that every father in America dressed that way when browning hamburger meat. We have already noted that the dominant culture sets the standard against which one measures incongruity. Obviously, contemporary America and biblical Israel or the early church do not share the same cultural frame of reference. In order to "get" biblical humor, it may be that we will find it necessary to make the effort first to put ourselves into the mind-set of biblical culture in order to perceive incongruity, to get the humor.

One almost insurmountable difficulty relates to the fact that humor, in its most native form, is not a literary phenomenon. Literary humorists, people who can be funny on a page, as it were, must compensate for the fact that humor depends heavily on sight and sound. Comedians depend on the ability to control the pace of their delivery, that is, they depend on their sense of "timing"; they often employ accents, voice characterizations, inflections, emphases, and the cadence of their speech to embody humorous incongruity, which is why some people are notoriously incapable of telling a joke. The problem is not with the words they use but the way they use them. Often, humor also depends on what we see: gestures, facial expressions, pratfalls, costumes, props, interactions between characters, etc. How does one translate timing or a particular intonation to the page of text? How does one make the situation and actions described in a text come alive in one's imagination like staging a play in one's mind?

All of these difficulties in conveying humor in texts are compounded, with respect to humor in the Bible, by the fact that neither the ancient Hebrew of the Old Testament nor the *koine* Greek of the New had yet developed systems of punctuation. That's right, the early manuscripts of the

Bible had nothing equivalent to periods, commas, or question marks. Early Greek manuscripts did not even have spaces between the words, and Hebrew manuscripts were written in a kind of shorthand without vowels until the seventh to ninth centuries CE! Even in English, however, our minimalist system of punctuation primarily reflects grammatical categories and syntactical structures and has virtually no ability to suggest tone, cadence, or emphasis. Consider all the freight that an English exclamation point has to carry. As written in the exclamation "Wow!" the punctuation indicates fervency and feeling, but what kind of fervency and feeling? Anger? Amazement? Disappointment? Anticipation? Appreciation? I invite the reader to experiment with the varieties of meaning implied by various emphatic pronunciations of this single word. Try saying "wow!" as though you had just seen the most handsome young man or beautiful young woman—whichever is appropriate—and were expressing to yourself appreciation for physical beauty; now try saying "wow!" as though you had just completed your federal income tax form and discovered how much you owe this year. The word is the same, and the fervor it expresses may be of equal intensity, but its meaning varies significantly depending on the tone and inflection used in pronouncing it.

Humor in the Bible? Why, of Course!

By the same token, it is important to recognize why the authors of the Bible might have been interested in employing humor in the first place. Once again, humor scholars offer some assistance. Studies have identified three general ways in which people use humor. First, in keeping with its "truth-telling" character, people sometimes use humor in aggressive, critical, subversive ways to point out incongruities to which people may otherwise be blind or which they may have an interest in actively denying. In our culture, political humor often functions in this way. Late-night comedians translate a president's human foibles into symbols of failures of leadership. If a dad can get his daughter to laugh at the spaghetti sauce covering her face, tacitly admitting that her habit of "slurping" up the noodles is unattractive, he may be able to get her to take seriously her need to improve her table manners. Second, humor can have a social function, including or excluding people in the circle of those who share the view of incongruity implicit in the humor. If you do not get the joke, it indicates that you do not see the world the same way the joke-teller does and vice versa. The joke, once told, acts like a spotlight revealing where hearers belong in relation to the joke, the joke-teller, and the social framework that defines both. For good or ill, ethnic humor falls into this category. Finally, humor can be used as a defense to sublimate fear or discomfort, to manage the incongruity. The men in my father's family typically go bald. One of my favorite great-uncles used to say, "God loves Biddle men so much that he gave them one pretty face and cleaned off a place for another." Thereby, he deftly acknowledged the problem, defused it, and transformed it into its opposite. So-called "gallows humor" typifies this use.

Given the apparent universality of humor in human life and its centrality to the healthy functioning of individuals and societies, it is almost inexplicable why it has taken readers and scholars of the Bible so long—millennia, in fact—to open their eyes to the presence of humor in the Bible. Anecdotal evidence suggests that a major factor hindering the recognition of humor in the Bible may be an assumption or bias dominant in contemporary culture, at least among some believers. I regularly receive hate mail, both in the post and electronically, from people who think that I am "making fun" of Holy Scripture in the seminary course I teach. Incidentally, I keep a file of these correspondences, just in case law enforcement should ever need them. My family and colleagues know where to find it, if anything unusual ever happens to me. Our culture has instilled in us an appropriate reverence for the Bible, but sometimes that reverence extends inappropriately to an attitude toward the Bible that threatens to deny its basic character.

I reiterate that I have no interest in "making fun" of the Bible, in turning the Bible into a comic book. On the other hand, with regard to the incongruity that is the core of humor, it is important to remember from the outset that the Bible is the record of God's historical relationship with God's *people*. Here is the operative word. People, individually and collectively, are inherently incongruous. People are funny—even God's people. My principal in middle school used to say that people have more fun than anybody. It's that simple. Should we be surprised that there are characters in the Bible who, like you and me, do some pretty incongruous things?

It all boils down to the notion that, in order to recognize something as incongruous, one must first have a sense of congruity; in order to recognize that something is out of the ordinary, one must be aware of the norms. In this light, humor, a sense of the comic, is serious business indeed. Even a slight chuckle indicates that one has recognized that something is out of kilter. In order to make that recognition, one requires a sense of what *ought* to be. Humor, then, has *a prophetic or a truth-telling dimension*. It makes one aware that one has confronted a truth that underlies the incongruity one has in view.

My maternal grandmother was a big part of my life. She was a character: vain in many positive ways but self-effacing in many others, down to earth, and with a rapier-sharp sense of humor. I can remember several occasions during my teen years when she did psycho-emotional surgery on me with it, lovingly but pointedly. My grandparents lived in town at the foot of the mountain, just where the road began its way up to the rural community where I grew up. Often, on the way home from work or school, I would stop by just to say "hello" and maybe to have a piece of Granny's fresh apple cake. I remember several occasions when, having left her, I would be driving up the mountainside, chuckling to myself about some story or joke she had told me, or about some pun or wisecrack she had coined, only suddenly to stop chuckling when I realized that she had been *lovingly* "making fun" of *me!* Did she just imply that my stubborn streak reminds her more of my dad than my hairline does? Because it was couched in humor, however, and especially because, more often than not, she had been on the mark, I usually took her correction to heart—or tried to do so. I will not say "always"; I was a teenager, after all. Still, she made me laugh about myself, and she was my grandmother who loved me and I knew it, so it had effect. I usually tried to fix or change whatever she had called to my attention, especially since she cared enough and had been wise enough to circumvent my adolescent insecurity with humor. She could get to me. No one wants it to be possible for one's grandmother to make a joke out of them. So I encourage people generally to be aware that laughter is often a clue that one has just acknowledged some incongruous truth, usually about oneself.

The Bible contains humor, I think, because it tells the story of real *people*. Real people are funny, and they are so because they are incongruous. The Bible has truth to tell that can be told more effectively by humorously calling attention to human incongruity than by preachy, pompous, propositional prose. This pertains, especially, to characterization. Few if any who read these words will have met my grandmother, of blessed memory, but, based solely on the story I related, you probably have begun to formulate an idea of what kind of person she was. It is common for someone to describe another person through stories rather than propositions. A *curriculum vitae* lists data, but it does not characterize a *person*. No list of factoids about me (favorite color: purple; eyes: blue-gray; hair: yes, I still have some, graying like the men in my mother's family) approximates getting to know me. Incidentally, one of the ironies of the current "social networking" fads such as Facebook, Twitter, etc. involves the substitution of data bits and blurbs for true human interaction—but I digress. If you ask my wife to characterize me, she will probably tell you stories about moments in my life that reveal much more than a list of factoids ever could. Likewise, the Bible tells the *story* of God's relationship with God's *people*. Therefore, rather than being surprised that it contains humor, we should expect it to do so.

Procedure and Plan

In the pages to follow, I will attempt to illuminate the humorous elements in several biblical texts. In order to overcome, perhaps with some degree of success, the problem of language and culture that separates contemporary readers of the Bible from its original setting, I will rely principally on two techniques: paraphrase and supplementation. Many examples of biblical humor occur in narrative texts, in stories. Many of these probably originated as oral accounts, as stories passed from generation to generation, similar in several ways to the family stories Granny used to tell me. In the effort to bring the humor of these biblical stories back to life, then, retelling them *as stories* seems to be the most suitable approach. Because of the difficulty in translating humor, however, and—at least for a professor accustomed to writing for academic audiences—in writing *about* humor in a way that will not, in fact, get in the way of the humor, I will try to find language, settings, and situations in contemporary experience that can serve as approximations, parallels, or paraphrases of the original. One might think of Sheriff Taylor retelling the biblical stories to Opie, Barney, and Aunt Bee.

At the other extreme, I sometimes find that it is necessary to pause in the retelling and supplement the account with background information about ancient Israelite or early Christian culture and institutions, geographical and historical details, or niceties of the Hebrew or Greek languages. One might think of a scholar on the American South explaining Sheriff Taylor's accent and figures of speech to a foreign exchange student from Germany. Because I value the integrity of the biblical text, I have tried to make clear to readers the difference between dialogue and narrative quoted from the Bible in translation (typically either the RSV, the NRSV, or my own translation from the original) on one hand, and dialogue and narrative that I have either paraphrased or, in some cases, imagined as probable implications of the actual text of Scripture on the other. These paraphrases and supplementations appear in *italics*. The Bible invites such exercises in sacred imagination and supplementation; it calls for readers to become engaged in the biblical story. It is important to distinguish, however, between what I think or anyone else thinks that the biblical story implies or suggests and what it actually says. Only the latter has scriptural authority.

At this point, a disclaimer is in order. In this book, I contend that the Bible contains humor, and I try to illuminate examples of it. Along the way, my comments *about* humor in the Bible may themselves be funny. I surely hope so. My primary goal, however, is not to write comedy but to alert readers of the Bible to the Bible's inherent humor, to equip them with the major tools necessary for recognizing this humor on their own, and to reflect on the theological implications of humor for a life of faith. I apologize in advance for the fact that, sometimes, explanations of the humor in the Bible are not themselves funny. Everyone knows the danger that explaining a joke may render it humorless. I will have succeeded only if, after you read my elucidation of the humor in a text, you are able to read that text itself with new eyes. The objective is not to attract attention to my comic skill but to refocus attention on Scripture!

After all, I am not a professional comedian. I am a teacher by vocation and a Baptist by confession. Both of these elements of my identity find expression in this book. It is not possible in a single book for me to explore every example of humor in the Bible, even assuming that I had identified and understood them all accurately. My intention, instead, is to help readers understand important examples of humor in the Bible and thereby (and even more importantly) to sharpen readers' sensitivities to the humor that abounds in Scripture. As a Baptist, after all, I do not presume to offer the "authoritative" interpretation of biblical texts. Rather, I hope to encourage and equip believers for a broader and deeper engagement with the Bible. I hope to open new vistas.

In sum, because humor does not translate easily or well across cultures, in the case of the Bible, especially since not only language but also time and place are involved, we have to work to "get it." The following retellings of several examples of humor in the Bible can be viewed as aids to "getting it." Once we have gotten it, perhaps its truth will motivate us to change our lives, to become more *congruous* with the reality of the kingdom of God.

The book consists of six chapters, each examining the biblical accounts of episodes in the lives of important figures: simpleton Isaac, the momma's boy and accidental patriarch; rascal David, the what-you-see-is-not-what-you-get king of Israel; satirist Esther, the cocktail-party queen, who exposes the powerlessness of empire; reluctant Jonah, the petulant prophet who succeeds despite his comical efforts to fail; debater Jesus, who outwits the brightest minds of his day but also provokes their determined opposition; and clueless, clownish Peter, who cannot see for looking. A final chapter will summarize what we have observed and comment on why it is important to recognize humor in the Bible in the first place. Because I hope that some readers will want to investigate humor or the comic phenomenon further—either generally or humor in the Bible specifically—I include a basic list of books and articles "For Further Reading." The sources vary widely from the profoundly technical to the popular. Readers may note that Old Testament figures seem to dominate the six chapters constituting the core of this book (by a margin of four to two). While I specialize in Old Testament, my specialty is not the reason for this apparent imbalance. Rather, it reflects the circumstances that the Old Testament contains a greater proportion of narrative than does the New Testament and that the Old Testament represents a greater proportion of the Bible. The ratio should not, therefore, be taken either as evidence that humor is more common in the Old Testament than in the New or that I have favored my area of particular expertise.

Finally, the arrangement of the book reflects the order of these stories in the Bible, but each chapter can stand on its own, so readers need not read it in order.

Chapter 1

How Isaac Got a Wife without Even Trying

"I've always thought that a big laugh is a really loud noise from the soul saying, 'Ain't that the truth.'" (Quincy Jones)

The Bible begins with the account of God's creation of the "very good" world, but the downward spiral of human history quickly follows: the first pair's overreaching, the first murder (a fratricide), the flood, the tower of Babel. Within the first eleven chapters of Genesis, humanity, divided now by language, is scattered across the earth, and it seems that God's original, good design has been hopelessly marred, if not ruined. If the Bible were a tragedy, it might well have ended with the flood and without Noah. Who could blame God for abandoning humanity to its evil intentions? The biblical story is not a tragedy, however. It surprises with the incongruous determination of God to persist toward God's original purpose, a good world. It surprises even more with the incongruous means God chooses for moving forward—by working through one couple on a migration from Mesopotamia to Syria and finally to Canaan.

The story of Abraham, the recipient of God's promise that he would be the ancestor of a great nation that would in turn be the avenue of blessing "for all the families of the earth" (Gen 12:3), hinges on the problem of the birth of the promised child. At the beginning of the biblical account concerning Abraham, we learn that he (12:4) and Sarah (cf. 17:17) are both already quite old (seventy-five and sixty-five, respectively) and, more important to the course of their story, childless (11:30). If they were to become the ancestors of a great nation, as God promised, the obvious starting point was to become the parents of one son.

Next: Abraham Needs Grandchildren but Isaac Is Not Cooperating

First things first. Readers of the Bible know the story of how everything unfolds, in fits and starts, over a long period: Abraham seemed at first to view his nephew, Lot, as his heir (see Gen 12:4-5), and when Lot left (ch. 13), his slave Eliezer seemed right for the role (15:2). Then Sarah gave Abraham her servant, Hagar, as a concubine. Consequently, Hagar became the mother of Ishmael, Abraham's biological son (but not Sarah's). Along the way, Abraham twice put the promise at risk by virtually giving Sarah to foreign rulers (12:10-20; ch. 20). By Genesis 24, the son, Isaac, has been born (21:1-7) and has survived the challenge to his status in the family that Sarah felt was posed by the presence of his half-brother, Ishmael, in the household (21:8-21) as well as the threat to his very life posed by the test of Abraham's faith (ch. 22). Genesis 24, the story of how Isaac got a wife without even trying, is the longest chapter in the book of Genesis (sixty-seven verses) and occupies a pivotal but sometimes under-appreciated position in the overall story of Israel's ancestors and the perpetuation of the promise. A summary of roughly the first sixty verses will set up the humor that surfaces at the end. In most contexts, after all, the "punch line" appears at the end.

Genesis 24 does not tell us, but we can deduce from the surrounding context that, by the time of the events recorded here, Isaac was, in fact, *forty* years old and unmarried, with no record that he even went to the prom in high school, as it were. Now, Abraham erroneously thought he was dying. Ironically, Isaac would also later take to his deathbed prematurely (Gen 27:2). Both lived many years after the false alarms; indeed, Abraham would marry again, a woman named Keturah, who would bear him six more sons (25:1-2). Nonetheless, Abraham thought that he was dying, and, taking account of things, he recognized that the promise that he would become the ancestor of a great nation was still in danger because, although he had the promised son, this son was forty years old, unmarried, and apparently had little interest in or initiative for marriage. One son does not constitute a great nation. First things first, of course, but there must also be second and third things in good order. The fulfillment of God's promise to Abraham required grandchildren, great-grandchildren, and so on. If Abraham and Sarah were to become the ancestors of a great nation, the family lineage could not end with Isaac.

Abraham's Wish and His Servant's Plan

Given Isaac's inertia, Abraham seized the initiative. He called in a servant, perhaps Eliezer although he is not named, and tasked him with finding Isaac a wife: *"I really don't want Isaac marrying one of these Canaanite girls from around here. I'd rather he took a wife from back home. So I want you to go back to Haran, where we came from, and I want you to promise me that you'll bring back a young woman to be Isaac's wife"* (Gen 24:2-4).

Wisely, the servant objected. He could not in good conscience make such a promise because he knew that he could not guarantee that he would find someone suitable or that she and her family would agree to the arrangement. He could not simply come riding into town and seize whomever he saw fit. When Abraham acknowledged that the servant had a point, the servant promised that he was willing to try. Abraham agreed that his desire would be satisfied if the servant promised to make a sincere effort.

After the ancient equivalent of shaking hands on the deal, the servant loaded ten camels with provisions and gifts for the prospective bride and her family and set out for Haran in Syria (the same place in both ancient and modern times). Just as the servant rode into town with this caravan, he belatedly realized the full difficulty of his task. Haran was a walled city during most of the second millennium, which is to say that it had a significant population. Conceivably, there were likely tens, scores, maybe even hundreds of young women of marriageable age and appropriate status suitable to be Isaac's bride. *"I should have thought this through,"* the servant must have realized. *"How am I going to make this determination? Am I going to hold a contest for the opportunity to be Isaac's wife? Shall I take out an ad in the Ancient Near Eastern equivalent of the newspaper or post one on the Ancient Near Eastern Internet?"*

Since, apparently, he could think of no practical means of making the choice, he decided to rely on God. *"God,"* he prayed, *"I will ask for a drink of water. Let's let the young woman who, in response, offers to water my camels as well be the one you have chosen for my master Isaac"* (Gen 24:12-14).

This proposal was quite sensible in many ways. The well was a center of commercial and social activity. Many, if not most, of the women in town would have visited the well in the course of a day. Abraham's servant would have the opportunity to review virtually all the candidates. He would simply sit at the well and be a girl-watcher until the right one came along.

A Prospect

The servant rode to the well just outside town, "parked" his camels, prayed this prayer, (v. 11) and, with that settled, Rebekah came along almost immediately. The servant asked her for a drink; she responded politely, and, as if she knew the script, she offered to water his camels as well. The Bible says that the servant sat watching Rebekah water the camels to see whether she would fulfill the terms of the arrangement he had worked out with the

Lord. Now, the servant's plan and the fulfillment of it, while sensible in many respects, was also quite ridiculous and incongruous—that is to say, humorous—in at least one important respect. Here, modern Western readers of the Bible run headlong into one of the typical obstacles to "getting it." Few such readers of the Bible are familiar with ancient wells or with the proper care and feeding of camels. Whereas for ancient readers the image was probably vivid—they were able to see events unfolding in their minds in some detail—modern readers see no incongruity here because they do not know the norms.

What was involved in watering camels? A typical camel can drink up to forty gallons of water in one trip to the trough. Rebekah transported the water, drawn by hand from the well and perhaps carried up a short flight of stairs (see v. 16), to the watering troughs in five-gallon clay water jugs that she probably balanced on her head. The servant had ten camels. A gallon of water weighs eight and one-third pounds, a five-gallon jug nearly forty-two pounds. The math is relatively simple, but the result is staggering. In order to water all of the servant's camels, Rebekah had to make almost one hundred round trips between the well and the watering trough, carrying a total of more than four hundred gallons of water weighing more than 3,330 pounds or more than two and one-half tons!

To review, Abraham's servant asked Rebekah for a drink of water for himself. She not only gave this absolute stranger something to drink but also *volunteered* to water his ten thirsty camels. We might not immediately recognize what was involved in this project, but she surely knew from experience.

This vignette alone already conveys a great deal of information about Rebekah: she was generous, hospitable, perhaps a bit naive—the servant, after all, was entirely unknown to her—and, above all, hardworking. In fact, the text introduces a motif here concerning Rebekah that continues throughout the account. It says that she did all of this "hurriedly" (RSV, KJV, etc.), which is a solid translation of the Hebrew. Genesis 24 repeatedly observes that Rebekah acted "in haste, hurriedly." A careful reader will note this characterization of Rebekah. While it suggests her industry in this context, her tendency to act quickly may present a problem later in the story.

Remarkably, while she was hurrying to water his camels, Abraham's servant sat quietly, perhaps in the shade, observing. He did not offer to help—there is no record that he even engaged Rebekah in conversation, and the Bible in fact emphasizes that "he observed her in silence" (v. 21)—while she made the necessary one hundred trips between the well and the watering trough. How long did it take?

Female readers may well respond, "Just like a man!" A gentleman in the audience when I recently made a presentation about the humor in this account remarked that he had witnessed a similar incident while in the US Army in northern Africa during World War II. His unit came upon an oasis where a family was irrigating their crops. An Arab gentleman sat under the shade of a palm tree supervising a group of women, presumably his wives and daughters, as they did the work. There was a well and a system of irrigation ditches. They were busily pouring water, drawn from the well in large jars, into the ditches to water the crops. The veteran said that he motioned to the gentleman in such a way as to point out the contrast between his comfort and the labor of his wives and daughters, to which gestures the Arab householder merely laughed and gave the universal thumbs-up sign. Talk about incongruity!

In any case, after Rebekah finished watering the camels, the servant interrogated her as to her identity and family, gave her jewelry, specifically rings and bracelets, and mentioned that he needed lodging for the evening. She identified herself as Isaac's cousin, although she did not yet know that she had done so, and added that the servant would be welcome to lodge with her family. In contrast, she made no inquiries about his identity, the purpose of his visit, or the reason for his generosity. Did she regard it as a reward for watering the camels? Ancient Semitic customs and social expectations may not have been the same as contemporary Western practices, but Rebekah's openness to this stranger and to his gifts seems at least somewhat naïve, even dangerous. I certainly would not encourage my college-aged daughter to water a stranger's camels, accept jewelry from him, and invite him home to spend the night without at least making the effort to find out who he is. To be honest, I do not want her to water a stranger's camels at all, let alone accept jewelry from him! Indeed, if some stranger shows up at my door after giving my daughter jewelry, I will find out very quickly who he is and what he has in mind, but he certainly will not be spending the night!

The Proposition

Not so with Rebekah's family. She *hurried* ahead to her house to tell them the tale of this generous stranger. Rebekah's father was dead. Her older brother, Laban, now the head of the household, "ran" out to the spring to meet this man, to make good on Rebekah's invitation. Apparently, Rebekah came from a family of "hustlers."[1] At first, Laban made no effort to find out the details of the servant's business with Rebekah. Two techniques of Hebrew storytelling are evident here, and both contribute to the atmosphere of incongruity that grows as the story progresses. One technique is delay that builds suspense, in this case suspense that is itself incongruous. Probably because of ancient customs concerning hospitality, the invitation, once offered, could not be easily withdrawn. Furthermore, the needs and comfort of the guest must be afforded priority over the host's curiosity. Therefore, Laban brought the servant home, groomed the camels, provided for the servant and his entourage the necessary means to refresh themselves from their journey, and offered them food—all the while bridling his curiosity and, conversely, if we read carefully, stoking ours.

The other technique is artful repetition, one of the reasons Genesis 24 is so long. It, too, has the effect of delaying the outcome of the story, of slowing the pace and titillating the reader's imagination. Abraham's servant refuses to eat the food prepared for him until he has explained why he has come—a hint at his sense of urgency. He may have been in a hurry to get down to business, but the narrator was not. A modern narrator might simply summarize that Abraham's servant told Laban who he was and why he had come. Instead, the ancient narrator of Genesis 24 reports the servant's rehearsal of the whole story, from the start to that moment, in a nearly verbatim duplication of the first section of the story: *"My master Abraham has grown old. . . . He called me in and asked me to promise to get a wife for Isaac. I said, 'I cannot make such a promise; but I can promise to try.' Abraham said that that would be sufficient. . . . As I arrived just outside town, I thought . . . Rebekah said, 'I'll water your camels, too!' . . . rings and bracelets . . . 'stay at my house . . . .' So, here I am"* (Gen 24:24-48).

The servant concluded with the report that he had thanked God for leading him straight to Rebekah and asked, pointedly, whether Laban and his family were going to go along with God's solution to Abraham's problem!

Rebekah Accepts the Servant's Proposal of Marriage (Made at Abraham's Behest on Behalf of Isaac, who Presumably Knows Nothing about It)

Laban and family responded, in effect, *"Well, it sounds as though you and God have everything worked out. Why are you bothering to consult with us? Take her."* Abraham's servant was delighted. He gave everyone presents and said, *"Fine, then. I'd like to leave bright and early tomorrow morning. My master, Abraham, is not well. He thinks that he may be nearing the end. My errand is to deal with the last bit of unfinished business in his life. I would very much like to be able to assure him of my success so that he can go to his rest in peace"* (Gen 24:54).

Rebekah's family was *not* delighted. *"Whoa, whoa! Wait just a minute. This is the first we have heard about all this. We don't know you from Adam's house cat. You come riding up with your caravan and a tale about our relatives and some agreement you've worked out with God concerning our sister. And now you want to leave with her tomorrow? We need time to get accustomed to this. At the very least, we need time to give Rebekah a proper bon voyage party!"* (Gen 24:55).

Modern readers may need to be reminded at this point that journeys of such distances (it was nearly four hundred miles from Nahor/Haran to Hebron) required weeks, were expensive, and were very dangerous, and that Rebekah would be effectively bidding her family farewell, perhaps never to see them again.

"Let's see what Rebekah thinks," they said.

Rebekah's family explained the whole situation to her again and asked whether she was willing to depart the next day on this grand adventure. Readers will remember that she always acted hurriedly, and she stayed true to her character. She did not ask for time to consider; she did not ask to have time to say farewells; she did not ask for time to pack; shockingly, she did not even express any curiosity about her intended husband (Is he handsome? Wealthy? Industrious? Kind? How old?). *"Sure!"* she said, instead—and quickly.

The text says that the family immediately held an impromptu farewell celebration. Then, the next morning, Abraham's servant reloaded the camels, now unburdened of the goods he had brought along to Rebekah's family as wedding gifts (the purpose for the caravan in the first place), with Rebekah's belongings and her servants' things, and all of them headed out again southward, toward Abraham and Isaac—and Rebekah's future.

Isaac Gets a Wife

At long last, after the delay has built suspense and heightened the reader's expectations—surely something that has taken this long to narrate must have a truly significant outcome—the story reaches its conclusion (Gen 24:62-67), where, as with all good storytelling, we can indeed expect to find the climax. It is a good idea to slow down and pay careful attention to the details. "Now Isaac had come from Beerlahairoi, and was dwelling in the Negeb. And Isaac went out to meditate in the field in the evening . . ." (Gen 24:62-63, RSV).

We have already encountered one of the difficulties with trans-cultural humor in regard to the effort involved in watering ten thirsty camels. Now we meet a problem that relates specifically to the Hebrew language and the challenges of translation. Many English Bibles have a note on the word translated "meditate" in the RSV indicating that the "meaning of the Hebrew is uncertain" or something to that effect. The Hebrew verb used here in the story (*swh*) appears to be what scholars call a *hapax legomena*, a word that appears only once in the Bible. Of course, when a word appears only once, it is impossible to be certain of its meaning. Scholars must rely on contextual clues, etymology, or parallels in other related languages. The most one can hope for is to make a reasonable, educated guess as to the proper translation of such words.

As it happens in this case, a similar word (*syh*) appears in two other texts in the Bible (1 Kgs 18:27; Mic 6:14), and both of the Hebrew words in question closely resemble a word in other Semitic languages (Arabic *shh*, for example). These possible parallels to our *hapax legomena* all mean, to put it colloquially, "to answer the call of nature." Could that be what the Hebrew word in Genesis 24 means, too? Well, maybe. In any case, of the possibilities, it is the only suggested meaning based on likely linguistic evidence—a related language has a similar word that may be etymologically related to our otherwise unknown Hebrew word. Everything else seems purely speculative. Furthermore, it suits the context. In an era before toilets, and probably even before chamber pots, one likely reason a nomadic shepherd might leave his tent in the evening to go outside would be to relieve himself. Bathroom humor in the story of one of Israelite's patriarchs? Why not? For our purposes, it might be suitable simply to paraphrase "Isaac went out to do *something* in the field in the evening" and leave to our imaginations the question of what he went out to do. He was almost certainly not meditating, however.

Returning to the story, we do not get far before we encounter another translation issue: ". . . and he lifted up his eyes and looked, and behold, there were camels coming. And Rebekah lifted up her eyes, and when she saw Isaac, she alighted from the camel . . ." (Gen 24:64-65, RSV).

The NRSV translates the last phrase "she slipped quickly from the camel." The Hebrew original uses a verb that means "to fall." Rebekah "literally" *fell* off the camel when she first saw Isaac "doing something in the field." Of course, she did so "hurriedly." Rebekah does everything hurriedly.

Why? Why did Rebekah fall off her camel when she first saw Isaac as he was "doing something" in the distant field? The biblical storyteller paints a vivid picture here with great economy of words. Rebekah, Abraham's servant, and the whole entourage were riding along at the end of the day. They had not stopped to camp, presumably because the servant knew that they were nearing their destination. Why stop at nightfall for another night of camping on the trail when a few hours more would see them arrive home? Isaac was interrupted in whatever he was doing by the sight of a caravan topping the hill in the distance. At precisely that moment, Rebekah caught sight of Isaac in the field, doing whatever he was doing. She abruptly halted her camel and dismounted, apparently startled by what she had seen. What did she see? What caused this abrupt reaction? Regardless of what she saw, was her startled reaction positive or negative?

In a quick or cursory reading of the story, one might easily overlook this detail. It invites one to pause, to consider what may have been going on in Rebekah's mind. Hebrew storytelling rarely supplies the interior dialogue of characters in the way that modern narrative does. Consequently, readers must judge what characters think and feel—their motivations, fears, and desires—by their actions. Biblical characters reveal their thoughts, attitudes, and motivations in their behaviors. Often, in Hebrew storytelling, actions speak *instead of* words.

Are there any clues in Rebekah's behavior that indicate her thoughts? Something has gotten her attention—positively or negatively. At this point, unfortunately, yet another obstacle to understanding the dynamics of the account presents itself. The story relates a dialogue between Rebekah and the servant concerning the figure Rebekah has seen in the distance: ". . . and [Rebekah] said to the servant, 'Who is the man yonder, walking in the field to meet us?' The servant said, 'It is my master'" (Gen 24:65, RSV).

As described in the introductory chapter above, written language is artificial to a degree since it does not indicate the rhythm, inflection, pitch, or tone of the speech it reports. In English, for example, we use the exclamation point to suggest excited or emphatic speech, but there is a wide range of possibilities within this category: anger, desire, dismay, etc. (Remember the "wow!" experiment discussed earlier.) In the case before us, it is possible to read the exchange with a number of inflections. Most readers of the Bible are likely to use or hear in their mind's ear the measured rhythm and sonorous tone of the pious preacher. Yet Rebekah and the servant certainly did not speak this exchange in that way. I suggest two more likely options. In Hebrew, Rebekah's emphasis on *"that* man *over there"* strongly suggests that she did not casually or disinterestedly dismount. No, she "fell." To dismount from a camel, Rebekah would have required assistance.

Thus, Rebekah's question may have expressed dismay or even disgust: *"Who in the world is that guy? (Please don't tell me he's Isaac, my intended!)."* If so, the servant would probably have mumbled sheepishly or apologetically, *"Yes. I'm afraid it is my master Isaac."* Alternatively, Rebekah may have expressed satisfaction or even delight: *"Who is that fine specimen of manhood?"* If so, the servant would have proudly confirmed her hopes that, indeed, she had hit the jackpot in the husband-to-be category.

Rebekah probably fell from the camel for one of these two reasons: either her first impression of Isaac disgusted/dismayed her, or it delighted her. Which was it? Does the context offer any clues? The story itself does not call attention to an important piece of information that the broader context supplies, namely, the fact that Isaac was forty years old (Gen 25:20). We can only speculate, of course, but Rebekah was probably much younger, as young, perhaps, as fifteen. She had never been married, but then neither had he. In fact, we remember that Isaac had shown no initiative in the matter, the circumstance that drives the whole episode. His dying father had felt it necessary to send a servant to woo a wife for him because Abraham thought he was running out of time waiting on Isaac to act. Rebekah was young, beautiful, energetic; Isaac was forty. Was he balding? graying? paunchy? By forty, things start happening to the body; gravity and genes begin to exert their influence.

What was Rebekah thinking when, seeing Isaac for the first time, she "fell" off the camel? Was she regretting her hasty decision to return with Abraham's servant to marry this forty-year-old man? Maybe she replayed the conversation in her mind and realized her mistake.

"Are you willing to marry the son of this servant's master (sight unseen)?" they asked.

"Sure!" I said.

"Well, are you willing to leave with him tomorrow, bright and early?" they asked.

"Sure!" I said. Water his camels, indeed!

Was she thinking, *"What in the world have I done?"* or *"Praise God, who has blessed me abundantly in return for my industry and willingness to take risks and step out on faith! What a fine husband God has given me!"* By this point in the story, my curiosity is piqued. I really want to know. Anything that requires such length to narrate must be important.

Does the text give us any other clues? There are a few more verses left. We have not come to the end yet and, in Hebrew narrative as in most good storytelling, the point is going to be at the end. Let's read on, then.

"So she took her veil and covered herself" (Gen 24:65, RSV).

I confess that I do not fully understand the significance of this action. Evidence suggests that she did not veil herself because women in her culture were supposed to wear veils in the presence of men, as one might assume. After all, she had been traveling unveiled all this time in the company of Abraham's servant and his whole entourage. As far as I can tell, scholarly explanations are largely speculative. Some interpreters point to the Mesopotamian betrothal custom that involved the groom veiling his fiancée as a symbol of their engagement so that the veil functioned like an engagement ring does nowadays. Women typically removed the veil after the marriage. If Rebekah's veil served such a function in this story, the fact that she *veiled herself*, that is, that Isaac did not veil her, could be seen as a symbol of the fact that Isaac had played no active role in wooing her. In effect, she had gotten herself into this marriage, and she might as well give herself her own engagement ring, too. I suppose she could have asked the servant to turn around and take her back home instead. This reference to Rebekah's veil may be an important comment, in other words, but I am unsure of what its importance may be. In any case, the story continues: "And the servant told Isaac all the things that he had done. Then Isaac brought her into his mother Sarah's tent, and took Rebekah, and she became his wife; and he loved her. So Isaac was comforted after his mother's death" (Gen 24:67, NRSV).

That's right: "into his mother's tent." Some translations (RSV, for example) apparently find this bit of information embarrassing and (mis)translate simply "the tent," although the Hebrew clearly specifies that it was "Sarah's tent." The translators' embarrassment itself is an important clue. Why had forty-year-old Isaac never married and, evidently, never shown any interest in marrying? The text reminds us ever so subtly of Isaac's relationship with his mother, Sarah, and suggests an answer. Put bluntly, Isaac was apparently a momma's boy. He had no reason to marry; he had his momma. The reference to Sarah reminds us how she had banished Ishmael for behaving like Isaac's big brother; she had been a ferocious defender and advocate for her darling son, Isaac, born to her wondrously in her old age. She had doted on him. Genesis 23 records Sarah's death;

immediately thereafter—and only thereafter—Genesis 24 records the events associated with Isaac's arranged marriage to Rebekah. Had Sarah encouraged Isaac to remain single (*"None of these girls is good enough for you, son!"*) and, by smothering him with her devotion, simply hindered his maturation?

"Into his mother's tent." Honeymooning in Mother's tent? People sometimes ask whether this was the custom in ancient times. No, not so far as I am able to determine. Isaac's actions here were truly odd. "Comforted after his mother's death." Significantly, the story says not one word about Rebekah's feelings for Isaac. Isaac immediately shifted his love for his mother Sarah to his bride Rebekah, it seems.

Rebekah? Rebekah fell off the camel because she was stuck now. She had "hurried" into a marriage with a forty-year-old momma's boy. Talk about a pig in a poke!

Humor and Characterization: Isaac, the Momma's Boy

The ending answers all the questions: why Isaac was still unmarried (he did not need a wife; he had his mother), why Abraham had to take the initiative to procure a wife for his son (Isaac saw no need), why Rebekah was startled by the first sight her future husband (he was old!). The ending also points to the future. If one did not know the rest of the story of Isaac's life, one could already anticipate a number of developments. Who would "wear the robe" in this family—industrious, clever, hardworking Rebekah or the forty-year-old momma's boy? In fact, as the story of their life together unfolds, Rebekah proves to be the shot-caller, the playmaker. Indeed, scholars divide the Genesis account of Israel's ancestors into two major narratives, the story of Abraham and the story of Jacob. There is no extended "Isaac" account; there is no story in which Isaac is the main character. Scholars typically observe that Isaac only appears in Genesis either as Abraham's son or as Jacob's father. One might also add that he only appears as Sarah's son or Rebekah's husband, too. He is never his own man.

So What? Humor and Grace

In the context of the whole biblical story, this characterization of Isaac is significant. The humor reminds us of the complications involved in many marriages between "momma's boys" and strong women. A recent survey indicates, incidentally, that a significant majority of American women think that husbands should call their mothers no more than once a day. The details of the Isaac story may be unique to ancient Israelite culture, but the general phenomenon is well known even today. Abraham was old and sometimes slow to understand; Isaac was spoiled by his mother and traumatized by his father—we often fail to appreciate fully the impact that the aborted sacrifice of Isaac must have had on him psychologically. I would have been a momma's boy, too, if Daddy had once almost sacrificed me on a fiery altar. I can imagine that, after the sacrifice episode, had Abraham said to Isaac that the weekend was going to be free and asked whether he would like to go fishing, Isaac may well have replied, *"Is Momma going with us?"* I would not have gone away with father Abraham alone ever again. Apparently, the patriarchs were quite a bunch: this old guy Abraham, this momma's boy Isaac, and this scoundrel Jacob, whose very name, derived from a verb that means "to cheat, outwit, outfox, connive, scam," means "Cheat." These characters were the patriarchs of Israel.

What does this say to us? As we make our way through the Bible story, we encounter the old, the momma's boy, the cheat, the disobedient Saul, the rascal David, and other frail and faulty human beings—all but one of the people storied in the Bible are flawed, after all. My students often ask why God could not have picked someone who was not going to mess up this way. I remind them that the selection does not give God a good option. We often look back on the people whose lives are recorded in the Bible with a pious bias. "The God of Abraham, Isaac, and Jacob," the Bible says. God called saintly Abraham; God favored Isaac, Abraham's dearly beloved son; God changed Jacob's name to Israel. Surely these people behaved in ways we cannot possibly emulate. They were giants of faith. We have no hopes of attaining their level of holiness.

Not so. The Bible depicts for us people who are as flawed and silly—as *comic*—as you and I. The point is that God uses even a momma's boy like Isaac for God's purposes. We are without excuse. We cannot say that we are not quite the caliber of Paul or Peter, James or John. Yes, we are. It is not a question of worthiness or abilities; it is a question of response to God's call. It is a question of whether God can accomplish God's purposes even through flawed human beings. There is something to the aphorism "It's not about ability, but availability," after all.

The Bible becomes a much more human and accessible book when we read it with an eye to its humor. The people who populate the biblical story are not flat, monaural, monochromatic, monotonous cartoon caricatures; rather, they are complex, deep, stereophonic, polychromatic, and sonorous people. The Bible is not just about "back then," a culture foreign to us, and people who were holier than we are. It is about human beings. We know what mommas' boys are. We know what over-protective parents are. We know what troubled father-son relationships are. We know people without initiative and people who make hasty decisions. We probably belong to one of these categories ourselves, at least sometimes. The mode of transportation may have changed, but people have not. God certainly has not changed in God's determination to fulfill promises. God still uses clowns like us, despite ourselves, to God's glory.

Humor in the Bible? How Have We Missed It So Long?

In the end, of course, the presence of humor in the story of Isaac's marriage to Rebekah should come as no surprise. In Hebrew, his very name, *Yizhaq*, appears to derive from one of a family of similar words that all have to do with laughter and play. Isaac means "he laughed." In fact, with the exception of only two episodes in which Isaac appears (the sacrifice story and this account of his marriage to Rebekah), Genesis always places a pun on Isaac's name at the center of each episode in his life. Abraham "*zahaq-ed*"/"laughed" when God announced Isaac's impending birth. Later, Sarah overheard God renew the promise. The idea that she and Abraham could have a child seemed to her the most ridiculous thing imaginable. After all, she thought privately, Abraham was much too old for romance ("*If this stranger making such outlandish promises had seen Abraham trying to pitch the tent the other day, he wouldn't be so confidant of his prediction*"), and she was post-menopausal. As the RSV translates the narrator's quaint aside, "it had ceased to be with Sarah after the manner of women" (Gen 18:11). Little wonder her internal dialogue expressed itself outwardly in laughter. Only the absurdity of the argument that ensued between Sarah and the visitor (had Sarah discerned the visitor's identity?) surpasses that of the scenario the stranger outlined to Abraham and eavesdropping Sarah. In an exchange that reminds one of children squabbling in the back seat of the car on the way to school in the morning, Sarah and God dispute whether she had, in fact, laughed.

God: *Abraham, why did Sarah laugh at my promise?*
Sarah: *I did not laugh!*
God: *Yes, you did!*
Sarah: *Did not!*
God: *Did so! I heard you!*

When Isaac was actually born (Gen 21:6-7), Sarah laughed again at the practical joke God had played on her, anticipating that everyone who heard of the event would laugh along with her. Perhaps she anticipated the reactions to her explanations in parent/teacher conferences that she was Isaac's mother, not his great-grandmother.

The meaning of Isaac's name continues its central function in the story of his life. Sarah determined to be rid of Ishmael when she noticed the older boy "*zahaq*-ing"/"playing" with *Yizhaq*, her darling boy (Gen 21:9-10). Later, when he observed Isaac and Rebekah "playing" in a fashion not suitable for brothers and sisters, King Abimelech of Gerar recognized that Isaac and Rebekah were not, in fact, brother and sister, as Isaac had claimed, but husband and wife (26:8). The story of Isaac is the story of laughter and play, of comic absurdity, of God's wondrous way of doing incongruous things. Isaac's is the story of centenarian fathers and nonagenarian mothers laughing at God, of momma's boys who become patriarchs, and of God who is ever faithful to God's incongruous promise.

Note

1. As a mere accident of language, the English word "to hustle," which denotes hasty, hurried activity, also carries connotations of deceit that the Hebrew word used to describe Rebekah's activity in the biblical account does not. In colloquial use, "hustler" refers to a con artist. Coincidentally, however, Rebekah later demonstrated a willingness, in fact, to "hustle" her husband in the matter of the blessing meant for Esau but appropriated by Jacob (whose name means "cheat"). Later still, Rebekah's brother Laban and her son Jacob engaged in a contest of deceit, each trying to "hustle" the other in the business transaction involving the dowries for Rachel and Leah. The English term conveniently alludes to both of these elements of Rebekah's character; the Hebrew term does not.

Chapter 2

David: Israel's What-You-See-Is-Not-What-You-Get King

". . . whoever gives birth to useless children, what would you say of him except that he has bred sorrows for himself, and furnishes laughter for his enemies." (Sophocles)

"Laughter and tears are both responses to frustration and exhaustion. I myself prefer to laugh, since there is less cleaning up to do afterward." (Kurt Vonnegut)

Sometimes it is hard to know how to assess reality. Whether something is good or bad sometimes depends on whether one can see beyond the immediate to a deeper reality, whether one can recognize the likely effects of a given cause. Comedian Archie Campbell illustrated this ironic quality of life's experiences in a comedy routine titled "That's Good. No, That's Bad," which he often performed with a partner. Below is a transcript of a performance of the routine with the assistance of singer-songwriter Roy Clark from an episode of the 1970s variety show *Hee Haw*.

> Archie: Hey, I guess you heard about my terrible misfortune.
> Roy: No, what happened?
> Archie: Yeah, my great-uncle died.
> Roy: Oh, that's bad.
> Archie: No, that's good.
> Roy: How's come?
> Archie: Well, when he died, he left me 50,000 dollars.
> Roy: Oh, that's good.
> Archie: No, that's bad.
> Roy: How come?

Archie: When the Internal Revenue got through with it, all I had left was 25,000 dollars.
Roy: Oh, that's bad.
Archie: No, that's good.
Roy: How come?
Archie: Well, I bought me an airplane and learned to fly.
Roy: Well, that's good.
Archie: No, that's bad.
Roy: How come?
Archie: Well, I was flying upside down the other day and I fell outta the dern thing.
Roy: Well, that's bad.
Archie: No, that's good.
Roy: How come?
Roy: Well, when I looked down under me and there was a great big ole haystack.
Roy: Well, that's good.
Archie: No, that's bad.
Roy: How come?
Archie: Well, I got a little closer and I saw a pitchfork aimed right at me.
Roy: Well, that's bad.
Archie: No, that's good.
Roy: How come?
Archie: I missed the pitchfork.
Roy: Well, that's good.
Archie: No, that's bad.
Roy: How come?
Archie: I missed the haystack too.
Roy: Well, that's bad.
Archie: No, that's good.
Roy: How come?
Archie: Well, I bounced around a few minutes and an ambulance come and took me to a hospital.
Roy: Well, that's good.
Archie: No, that's bad.
Roy: How come?
Archie: Well, I was in the hospital there for a while and I took a turn for the nurse.
Roy: That's bad.
Archie: No, that's good.
Roy: How come?
Archie: Well, my wife came in one day and caught me kissing this nurse.

Roy: Oh, that's bad.

Archie: No, that's good. She said if that was the way I was gonna act I could have that pretty nurse, she was gonna pack her clothes and go back home to Momma.

Roy: Oh, that's good.

Archie: You're dern right that's good.

You probably know the story of David well but may never have noticed the ironic tone that runs throughout the biblical account of his life and career. David almost personifies the idea of "that's-good-no-that's-bad" incongruity. Chosen by God to be Israel's king and chosen by Saul to be court musician, David came to the attention of the Israelites when he defeated Goliath. These are good things. No, they are bad. All of these positives only resulted in Saul's negative, indeed murderous, reaction to David. That is certainly bad. No, it is good, because all of Saul's attempts to engineer David's demise backfired in Archie Campbell fashion. We will not attempt a comprehensive examination of the story of David's life. After all, it takes up half of 1 Samuel, all of 2 Samuel, and extends into 1 Kings. Instead, we will note the accounts of episodes in David's career that highlight the Bible's ironic portrayal of this incongruous figure.

An Ironic Figure

First, however, we should examine the concept of irony manifest both in Campbell's comedy routine and in the life of King David. Anyone who studies the story of David's career must struggle with the question of how to interpret it. Most of us in the pews come to David with Sunday school memories of the sweet but courageous shepherd boy killing Goliath, or we think of David, Israel's great psalmist, or we remember the famous passage that refers indirectly to David as the "man after God's own heart" (1 Sam 13:14). We tend, therefore, to have a positive view of him as a model of faith and piety. Yet the account that extends from 1 Samuel 16 through 1 Kings 2 is not nearly so positive. In fact, it is quite ambiguous; it is ironic.

Irony has three basic characteristics: (1) it involves two layers of reality; (2) it hinges on incongruity between the layers; and (3) it depends on someone being unaware of one of the layers (and by implication, someone else recognizing it).[1] Furthermore, irony occurs in two basic types: verbal (through what someone says) and situational (through what someone does). In one of the clearest examples of verbal irony in the Bible, for example, the priest Caiaphas infamously rebuked the other members of the Sanhedrin for their indecisive handling of Jesus: "You do not understand that it is better for you that one man should die for the people than to have the whole nation destroyed" (John 11:50, NRSV). Caiaphas meant that, unless they disposed of Jesus, they ran the risk of insurrection and a harsh Roman reaction to squelch the unrest. He argued for the pragmatic necessity of getting rid of Jesus. That's bad. No, that is ultimately good. Readers of the Gospel of John are likely to see a more profound level of truth in Caiaphas's statement. Caiaphas spoke the truth about Jesus' death to save a whole nation, indeed, the whole of humanity, even though the high priest had no inkling of what he had said.

Perhaps the most pointed example of situational irony in the Bible occurs when Tamar, Judah's daughter-in-law, presents him with his own signet ring, cord, and staff in answer to his question concerning the identity of the father of her unborn child, conceived, he thought, in promiscuity. How ironic that he should ask! He thought that he had caught her in an immoral act punishable, in that time, by death. He would finally be rid of this jinxed woman who had, he thought, cost him two sons. That's bad for Tamar. No, that's good for Tamar. It's bad for Judah. In the moment, he recognized the truth of the situation he had gotten himself into; he also recognized that, although he had thought Tamar guilty of adultery, in fact, he was the guilty one—guilty of deception, of dishonoring the memory of his oldest son, and of neglecting his daughter-in-law.

Irony falls under the heading of humor because of the element of incongruity. Like all humor, it is the recognition of a truth that need not be explicitly stated. It involves a number of roles: someone creates the irony, someone recognizes it, and someone does not. Students of irony sometimes call the one who creates the irony the "ironist." The participant who does not recognize both layers of reality is sometimes called the "victim," because he or she "is in the dark" about the deeper truth at hand and, therefore, cannot act with the full benefit of accurate knowledge. Indeed, this quality of irony accounts for the fact that it can often be very dark humor (witness Judah and Caiaphas). The identity of the one who recognizes (the "perceiver") can vary widely from an actor or speaker directly involved in the situation to a narrator, a reader, or a spectator standing outside the events. It is possible simultaneously to be both the ironist and the perceiver (or one of the perceivers). It is possible to be the ironist and fail to perceive the irony. Perception is the point. The one who does not "get it" or does not "get it" soon enough to avoid disaster fails the challenge irony presents. The truth-telling aspect of humor comes to center stage in irony. In irony, humor assumes perhaps its most serious, somber, sober form. It reveals Judah's hypocrisy and Caiaphas's cynicism. Most of all, perhaps, it asks hearers/readers/observers to look at themselves. Can we see the deeper truth, or is our vision shallow, our decisions incongruous with reality, our behaviors comically self-defeating?

Since we are talking about stories in the Bible, several sets of possibilities deserve our careful attention. We will want to pay attention, for example, to whether someone in the story recognizes the truth and, thus, reveals it to us. Alternatively, the narrator may know the truth and communicate it to us. In yet another possibility, the narrator or narrators may never tell us how we should view the events that they relate or what we should learn from them. In such a case, as with metaphors, one must construe the meaning of the irony; one must interpret it. Does the metaphor, "my lover's lips are like cherries," suggest that her lips are red, sweet, tart, fleshy, attractively rounded, juicy, some other cherry quality, or all of these possibilities at once? Inevitably, the hearer/reader must decide. Similarly, irony can suggest; it can point to the incongruity between reality and appearance, but, in order to succeed as a communication strategy, it must rely on the skillful attention of the reader/hearer. The David story, for example, includes no proverb, moral, or interpretive statement along the way to indicate that on balance we should see David positively or negatively. To the contrary, it overtly warns that, with regard to David, things are seldom as they seem (1 Sam 16:7). Since the David story does not explicitly guide our understanding of David, we will want to take great care to recognize irony and its significance ourselves, lest we become the "victim," stuck in the dark. Interpreting well will involve seeing through the merely apparent to the depth of reality in the David story. If we do not, the ironic "joke" may be on us.

God Sees Differently

Scholars divide David's life and career generally into four rather distinct periods. The first, the primary focus of this chapter, recounts David's rise to prominence, when he rises from shepherd boy, the youngest of Jesse's eight sons, to become son-in-law of the king. Along the way, Samuel anoints him the next king of Israel secretly and without fanfare. During the second period, David's fugitive period, the public still does not know that he has been anointed to be the next king, but his predecessor and eventual father-in-law Saul becomes both suspicious of David's election and jealous of David's success, and David must essentially run for his life. This period ends with Saul's death in battle and David's rise to power in probably the shortest period in David's career—the Bible certainly devotes the briefest narration to recount it. Finally, David's mature reign, the fourth period when he rules over Judah in the south and Israel in the north, proves to be somewhat disappointing. It turns out that, like many contemporary politicians, David is better at becoming king than he is at governing. But that is an issue for later.

The story does begin, however, with a clue that David's career will exemplify irony. After Saul spared the life of the Amalekite king, Agag, contrary to God's instructions, God told him, in effect, *"That does it. I'm tired of your disobedience and arrogance. I am going to replace you with someone better, with someone after my own heart"* (1 Sam 13:13-14). That's bad. No, that's good because, consequently, God told Samuel the prophet to go to Bethlehem to the home of a certain Jesse, and that among Jesse's sons Samuel would find the one whom God would choose to be the next king of Israel. Samuel did as God directed. When he arrived, he arranged for all of Jesse's sons—or supposedly all of Jesse's sons—to parade before him.

> When they came, [Samuel] looked on Eliab and thought, "Surely the LORD's anointed is now before the LORD." But the LORD said to Samuel, "Do not look on his appearance or on the height of his stature, because I have rejected him, for the LORD does not see as mortals see. They look on the outward appearance, but the LORD looks on the heart." (1 Sam 16:6-7, NRSV)

In other words, God said, *"Samuel, be aware, as I am, that there can be incongruity between appearance and reality."* Amazingly, the story of David begins with God's statement alerting Samuel, along with the readers of the Bible, that the contrast between appearance and reality will mark David's whole life and career. It seems that even God has an ironic sense of humor. In any case, readers of the story of David have now been given ample warning that the account to come will be rich in levels of reality, in misdirection, in layers of meaning—in short, in ironic humor. Obviously, all of the characteristics of irony apply to the situation described in this account of David's anointing as Israel's future king. No less a figure than God himself announces that David's reality is complex, and that what you see is not necessarily what you get. Incongruity? How could it be more pronounced? This shepherd boy was to be the king? At first, Samuel, Jesse, and all of Jesse's sons, presumably including David, did not see in David what God claimed to see.

Duly warned, let us proceed. Are we up to the challenge to see beyond the apparent to the actual, through the merely obvious to the real? Will we see the truth or fall victim to our superficial vision, as it turns out Saul did?

Samuel's vs. God's Perception of Reality

After Eliab, Jesse called each of his sons in turn to pass in review before the Lord (and Samuel): first Abinidab, then Shammah, and so on, until seven of his eight sons had presented themselves to the Lord (and Samuel). In turn, God rejected each of them—seven sons, seven rejections. Ironically, in Hebrew thinking, of course, the number seven represents perfection or completion. Could Jesse have been thinking that he had presented God with the "perfect" selection of sons from which to choose the next king? If so, he soon experienced "complete" rejection. Samuel knew, on the one hand, that God had sent him to find the next king among Jesse's sons but, on the other hand, that none of these seven strong young men had been chosen. That's bad. No, that's good. Surely, God was not mistaken; the mistake must have been Jesse's. Quite logically, Samuel asked Jesse whether he had other sons and learned that there was, in fact, an eighth. Jesse responded, *"There is yet the baby boy who's out with the sheep, but I didn't think he would be a good candidate; you know, he's just a kid. I didn't think you'd want to see him."* Samuel reasserted the original instruction: *"I said I needed to see all of them. Bring him in, too!"* (1 Sam 16:11).

The Bible's description of David is delightfully witty: "Now he was ruddy, and had beautiful eyes, and was handsome" (1 Sam 16:12, RSV, NRSV). Had not God just told Samuel that outward appearance does not matter, that he should not take account of it? Yet the first thing the narrator tells us about David is that he was a tanned, good-looking, kid-of-a-boy (as my granddad used to say) with pretty eyes! In Hebrew, his name is even related to a word that means "darling." This description provides enough information to excite the imagination but not enough information of the right kind to answer the question as to why David was a good choice for the throne. In fact, it sounds more like the way David's mother or grand-mother might have described him, especially the reference to his eyes. Although I doubt it, ancient Israelite culture may have differed from modern Western culture on this point, but at least in my experience, men do not usually remark on a boy's pretty eyes! The observation calls to mind a mother's view of her darling baby boy, not a prophet's image of the king of Israel. God had said that David's heart mattered, not his youthful good looks. What does the description of his physical appearance suggest about

David's character? Does it indicate that he had the fortitude, courage, wisdom, and experience necessary for leading a nation or, rather, that he was sweet, innocent, even naive, and kind?

The answer unfolds over the course of the next several episodes in the story of David that took place in the period of David's "rise to prominence." It establishes one pattern for becoming king in ancient Israel, the pattern later followed in the northern kingdom of Israel. A prophet privately anointed someone as king; then the people publicly ratified the selection of the anointed one. The two-stage process was a practical necessity: if anyone could get some prophet to anoint them with oil and thereby automatically become king, there would have been kings all over the place. Ancient Israel realized, as the church does with respect to callings to ministry and ordination, that if someone has a true calling, the community will recognize those gifts and endorse that calling. Recognition and ratification are the core meaning of ordination. One can imagine someone like David anointed, but unless, or in this case until, the people recognized God's call and presence in his life, he could not assume the throne. At this point Samuel had secretly anointed David, but if you had stopped the average Israelite on the street and said, "Do you think that sweet, good-looking, well-tanned, pretty-eyed young David is going to be a good king?" they would have answered, "Who is David?" In order to rule as king, David had quite a distance to travel. He must first become prominent enough for the people to recognize him as God's anointed. Ironically, they must discern from external appearances what God had seen in David's heart. The people must withstand irony's test of perception!

The Test Begins

How does that process of public discernment begin? Saul had already shown evidence of a troubled psyche. We would probably say today that he was bipolar or schizophrenic, or something; in any case, he was not a happy individual. The Bible says that in the same moment the Lord sent his spirit upon David (that's good), he sent an "evil spirit" upon Saul (that's bad). It also says that from time to time Saul "raved." Surely that's bad. No, that's good, because Saul's advisors concluded that they needed to do something about Saul's state of mind. They decided to try music therapy. It turns out—and now we have to add this to our picture of David—that David was not only a handsome, tan, pretty-eyed teenager but also a folk singer, apparently with some reputation. Therefore, Saul's advisors brought David to Saul's court, such as it was, to provide Saul with mood music or to be his music therapist. The image that comes to mind for me is Bobby Sherman or Shawn Cassidy; my students tell me they think of the youngest of the Jonas Brothers or Justin Bieber; some readers will think of Bobby Darin or the young Frank Sinatra.

Immediately after Saul's advisors summoned David to court, as the Bible tells the story, David began his job. "And whenever the evil spirit from God came upon Saul, David took the lyre and played it *with his hand* [how else?]. And Saul would be relieved and feel better, and the evil spirit would depart from him" (1 Sam 16:23, NRSV). The picture is almost complete: the teenage shepherd boy, with pretty eyes and a nice tan, who also has a sweet, probably tenor voice and can play the lyre, singing Saul's favorite folk song. The very image of a wise and effective king, is it not? At every stage in the David story, one must remember that it began by warning readers that appearances and reality are not going to correspond. There can be no question that the story begins in irony.

We can skip to the end of the David and Goliath episode, because, although it has humorous elements (the image of David, the twelve-year-old boy, decked out in Saul's armor that weighs him down, hangs loose, and entangles arms and legs, threatening to trip David as he walks, and that offers no effective protection anyway, is almost slapstick), the aftermath of David's victory over Goliath contains the first hint of David's future fame:

> As they were coming home, when David returned from killing the Philistine, the women came out of all the towns of Israel, singing and dancing, to meet King Saul with tambourines, with songs of joy, and with musical instruments. And the women sang to one another as they made merry, "Saul has killed his thousands, and David his ten thousands." (1 Sam 18:6-7, NRSV)

This brief account abounds in irony. First, it is important to note that the women celebrate. Second, although the text explicitly states that the women come out to greet King Saul, their victory song ironically culminates in a glorification of David. What's more, their song is a blatant exaggeration. How many had David in fact killed? One, certainly not "tens of thousands." Clearly, women adored David. Can you imagine what must have been in the heart of every Israelite girl and Israelite mother of daughters along the parade route? Young, sweet David was cute (*"Just look at those eyes, Miriam! Have you ever see such dreamy eyes?"*); he had a clear, beautiful tenor voice (he probably had a top ten on the pop charts by then); and now he was a military hero. He had killed that awful Philistine giant, Goliath. David was handsome, young, sensitive, and courageous. How many crushes were born during this victory parade? What son-in-law material he was! That's good.

Saul Fails the Discernment Test

No, that's bad. The real irony comes in the next two verses. The Bible says that when the women sang about the tens of thousands of Israel's enemies that their darling young David had slain, "Saul was very angry, for this saying displeased him. He said, 'They have ascribed to David ten thousands, and to me they have ascribed thousands; what more can he have but the king-dom?' So Saul eyed David from that day on" (1 Sam 18:8-9, NRSV). Without knowing it, Saul had asked the appropriate question. The narrator knew, and therefore readers already know, that Samuel had anointed David to be the next king. Samuel knew, of course, and so did David and, presumably, his family, but Saul did not. The women did not know. Yet Samuel had already told Saul that because of his mistakes and transgressions, God had tired of him and had "torn this kingdom of Israel from [him] this day and has given it to [his] neighbor who is better than you" (1 Sam 15:28, RSV), so he had good reason to be wary of rivals for his throne.

Did Saul suspect that David was such a rival? Did he see David merely as an ambitious young man or as a potential usurper? If the latter, then tall, strong, powerful King Saul would surely have been able to handle the threat posed by a boy singer. What if, however, there were more to the David story than Saul could see on the surface? What if God were behind David's freak-ish victory over Goliath and David's sudden and disproportionate popular-ity? If so, any overt effort to remove David as a potential rival would mean directly opposing God. David may have looked like ancient Israel's equiva-lent of a pop-idol boy singer, but there was obviously something intangible about the boy that suggested a promising future. Saul ought to have watched David closely, because in David's case, as we know, the relationship between appearance and reality can be tricky. Was David the "better" candidate for the throne of which Samuel had foretold? Despite the women's song, Saul knew that he had killed far more of Israel's enemies in battle than David had. Saul, however, did not know enough or did not want to know enough to be able to choose a wise course of action.

David Faces His Own Test

In point of fact, Saul did much more than simply "eye" David. The very next day, "an evil spirit from God rushed upon Saul, and he raved within his house, while David was playing the lyre, as he did day by day. Saul had his spear in his hand, and Saul threw the spear, for he thought 'I will pin David to the wall.' But David eluded him twice" (1 Sam 18:10-11, NRSV). The text begs the reader to envision the scene. In a foul mood, Saul sat on his throne, maybe brooding over Samuel's prophecy and David's popularity. He happened to have his spear in hand. Ruddy, cute, sweet-voiced, darling David sat against the far wall, supplying the background music, singing his "Best of David ben Jesse" medley perhaps. Suddenly, the king hurled his spear straight for David. I do not know what David must have thought. Maybe David thought, *"Okay, he doesn't like that one. How about something a little more upbeat? I've got that, I can do that."* Maybe he switched to some other song: *"This land is your land, this land is my land . . . ."* Perhaps David thought, *"I'll sure be glad when they invent remote controls, because this business of throwing the spear at me to get me to change songs is dangerous."* Oddly, David seems to have had his own difficulty distinguishing between appearance and reality. Most people would have rightly interpreted Saul's actions as attempted murder, but apparently David did not. That's bad. No, that's good because the text says that David eluded Saul twice and apparently continued singing. There will even be a third such incident later in the story (1 Sam 19:10; cf. 1 Sam 20:33; Saul was short-tempered).

"How many times do I have to throw a spear at you before you leave?"

"All right, fine! Get another singer, then. I'm not just going to sit here. You hired me as music therapist or human stereo, not as a bullseye for your target practice. I quit!"

Remembering that things may not be as they seem, it may be helpful to review what we know. We know who David is going to become, but who is young David at this point in his life? Innocent, even naive, or naively overconfident? No one, not even a king, is going to throw a spear at me more than once. I will leave or throw it back; I may throw it back and then leave, or throw it back as I leave; leaving, I may sneak around behind and then throw it. In any case, I am not simply going to continue playing and singing. Three times Saul threw his spear at David with the clear intent to kill him. The Bible says only that "Saul was afraid of David because the LORD was with him [that's good], but had departed from Saul [that's bad if you are Saul]" (1 Sam 18:12, NRSV). We do not know what David thought about the whole chain of events to this point. The Bible leaves it to us to imagine.

The Irony Deepens . . . and Darkens

At this point, Saul could have opened his eyes to the obvious signs that David enjoyed God's special favor. Instead, Saul's behavior only assumed an increasingly ironic flavor. On one hand, spurred by his dark mood, he made overt efforts to spear David. In more reflective, temperate moments, he devised plans to rid himself of David more subtly. After all, Saul did not know for sure what David had in mind or who he was in God's eyes. In order to eliminate the threat he perceived in David, Saul needed what is nowadays called "deniability." Saul needed to engineer a situation in which David was likely to die a death that could not be directly attributed to Saul. In other words, although the text does not say so, Saul was now wary of the possibility that David might be God's protégé. Consequently, based on David's vast military experience (killing one Philistine), Saul commissioned David as an officer in the army. Saul must have reasoned that tending sheep and taking one lucky shot with the sling had not prepared David for leading troops into battle. David would probably make serious strategic and tactical mistakes. The odds were that David would die in battle. That's bad.

No, that's good. As the story unfolds, of course, everything Saul attempts backfires, because, ironically, as Saul correctly suspected and as David knew and the reader knows, God was on David's side. Of course, therefore, when Saul commissioned David and sent him out to fight the Philistines, inexperienced David did not die in battle as Saul hoped. Rather, David enjoyed great success, presumably not because of his military skill and experience but because God was with him. In fact, Saul's plan backfired in an entirely unintended consequence. David not only gained the skill and experience he lacked and would need to rule as Israel's king but also became even more popular with the people. All the while, his reputation in Israel grew. That's good.

No, that's bad. Saul's spears had failed to kill David and the Philistine army had failed to kill David for Saul, so Saul resorted to a tried-and-true tactic—marriage. As they say, these days half of all marriages may end in divorce, but the other half end in death. In Saul's day, the statistics favored the second option, and Saul meant to hasten the outcome.

Saul hit on the idea of offering the hand of Michal, his younger daughter, in marriage (1 Sam 18:20). The episode reminds me of junior high school romances. Rather than talking personally with David, Saul had his people talk to David's people about whether or not David would be interested in marrying Michal. *"Michal's sweet on David; does David like her back?"* David sent word to Saul through intermediaries that he would, in fact, be amenable to the idea but that he was poor and did not have the means to pay a dowry. Word came back to David that something could be arranged, and David agreed. Saul proposed an interesting substitute. *"I'll tell you what I'll do. I won't insist on a formal marriage dowry. I am willing to settle for one hundred Philistine foreskins."* David quickly agreed to these terms.

Had Saul changed his mind about David? Had he decided that, since he could not best David, he may as well welcome David into the royal family? Hardly. The text explains Saul's reasoning: "Now Saul planned to make David fall by the hand of the Philistines" (18:25b, NRSV). Saul thought that he had finally lured David into a trap. What was David going to do, take out an ad in the Philistine papers? *"Young Israelite boy has the opportunity to become prince of Israel. Needs 100 Philistine volunteers. Please apply in person."* No, David would have to kill one hundred Philistines, one by one, in order to meet Saul's requirement. Saul expected, quite understandably, that David might be successful once or twice, but Saul could count on Philistine men to resist pretty strongly under these circumstances. Surely, some big, mean old Philistine was going to break David's neck. At least Saul hoped so. Of course, we know something that Saul did not. God was on David's side!

The Bible reports the denouement tersely and straightforwardly. "David rose and went, along with his men [David had men by now; Saul failed to take that into account, too] and killed [the Hebrew Bible says 100, the Greek text says 200] of the Philistines, and brought their foreskins, which were given in full number to the king" (1 Sam 18:27, NRSV). I imagine this scene vividly. David returned with a bag or a bucket of Philistine flesh and presented it ceremoniously to the king, announcing that it was all there, "in full number." I imagine David suggesting that Saul could count them if he wanted to be certain. I can also imagine Saul's response: *"No, that's okay. I'll take your word for it."* Alternatively, he may have turned to one of his staff, somehow in disfavor, and commanded, *"George, count them."* I also imagine George resigning rather than suffering the humiliation. This episode involves vulgar, rude, crude, almost juvenile humor. Ultimately, however, Saul gave David Michal's hand, they were married, and that was the end of that business. The outcome finally brought Saul to the recognition that the Lord was on David's side (1 Sam 18:28). That's good? Poor Saul could not win for losing.

Finally, Saul Sees the Truth—and Rejects It

What could Saul have done? After Jonathan (Saul's son, David's brother-in-law and best friend) interceded on David's behalf, there was a brief period of relatively smooth relations between Saul and David (1 Sam 19:1-8). But then, again, "an evil spirit from the LORD came upon Saul, as he sat in his house with his spear in his hand; and David was playing the lyre" (1 Sam 19:9, RSV). Whatever else one may say about Saul, he did not give up easily. The third spear attack failed to kill David, just as the first two had failed. The Philistine army had failed, and one (or perhaps two) hundred Philistine men had failed. Better planning and more direct action seemed necessary. Therefore, Saul sent a party to ambush David in his bed. That's bad.

No, that's good. Jonathan and David's wife Michal (Jonathan's sister) learned of Saul's plan and undertook to thwart it. They put a statue in David's bed, dressed in David's clothes with a goatskin on its head, evidence that David of the ruddy complexion also had plenty of reddish hair. Meanwhile, David fled to Samuel at Naioth in Ramah, and the ambushers reported what they found in David's bed to a disappointed Saul, who had the nerve to complain to Michal that she had deceived him!

The next episode illustrates the degree of Saul's desperation. He sent "messengers to take" David from Naioth, but when they approached the band of prophets associated with Samuel, the spirit of prophecy overtook them and they fell into a prophetic frenzy. A second and third embassy had the same experience. Frustrated, Saul went himself to capture David, only to experience a prophetic ecstasy that left him lying naked for a day and a night and that brought him infamy in Israel: "Is Saul also among the prophets?" (1 Sam 19:24). *"If he were, would that be a good thing?"* Poor Saul could not win for losing; God was on David's side.

Amazingly, in a conversation with Jonathan, after all Saul's efforts to kill him, David still expressed a willingness to return to Saul's court. Although events have made it clear to even a casual reader and although the narrator obviously understood Saul's purposes, Jonathan and David entertained the possibility that the whole thing had been a misunderstanding! At least they had learned to be cautious. Jonathan and David agreed that, before David returned to court, Jonathan would attempt to discover his father's true intentions toward David. They made an appointment to meet after Jonathan investigated. Jonathan outlined the plan:

> *Let me tell you what I will do. I'll go home, and I'll take a few days and talk to some of Dad's advisors and have a conversation or two with him, and I'll*

be able to tell the general tenor of his attitude toward you. Either he sincerely loves you as his son-in-law and my friend and appreciates everything you've done for him and for Israel, or these incidents have not been accidents or mis-understandings. Surely, I'll be able to find out which it is. But we need to take precautions. We can't meet like this publicly. He may be having me followed to see whether I will lead him to you. So, when I've done this, I'm going to meet you a week from next Thursday out by that big rock—you know where it is. You hide behind it. I'm going to bring my bow and arrow and a servant boy. Ostensibly, I'm going to take target practice. And after I've shot all the ar-rows in my quiver, I'll send the servant out to fetch and return them. At that point, I will say to him either, "No, no, I shot them farther than that. You need to go on a little farther." That will be the sign to you—one if by land, two if by sea—that you need to run away, get out of here. Otherwise, I will say to the servant boy, "No, no, I didn't shoot them that far. They fell closer. Come back this way." That will be your sign that you can come back to court. (1 Sam 19:18-23)

Jonathan probably wanted to use this code in case Saul was having him followed. He did not want to present Saul with the opportunity to capture and kill David. Jonathan gathered the necessary information, assuring him-self that Saul wanted nothing more than he wanted David dead. At the appointed time, then, he went out to the field by the designated rock, and he did everything just as he had said he was going to do. He shot his arrows; he sent the young boy out to fetch them; and he said, *"No, no, they have gone farther than that,"* the signal that David was in extreme danger and should flee secretly and immediately. What did David, in fact, do? Incredi-bly, David stepped out from behind the rock and said, *"So, you think I need to run away, do you?"* Rather than steal away quietly, David exposed himself in the open field to any ambush Saul may have arranged. That's bad. No, that's good. We might observe that David was lucky that Saul was not as clever as Jonathan thought he might be. Otherwise, we might conclude that God protected naive David—and, perhaps, that David had begun to rely, even to presume, on that protection.

In the end, however, David went into hiding, launching the next phase in his life: his so-called "fugitive period." This turning point offers a splendid opportunity to assess whether and how God's hint that, where David is con-cerned, things are not what they seem, has proven valid. If one considers David later in his life—the David who wooed Abigail away from Nabal and killed Uriah to conceal his affair with Bathsheba—one would hardly char-acterize him as innocent and naive. Much to the contrary, he was shrewd, calculating, cold, self-centered, even ruthless. At this point in his life, however—as a married man and an experienced military commander—he seems just as trusting, accepting, naive, and innocent as he had been when he was the shepherd boy singing folk songs for the king. Bless his heart. He behaved as though he thought he was invincible. Thank goodness Jonathan said, *"What are you doing stepping out into the open this way? You are going to get killed. Get out of here, quick!"* and David escaped. Poor Saul. Responsibility for the great failure to perceive and accept the reality underlying appearance belongs, of course, to Saul. Despite David's God-given good fortune in the face of adversity and despite the general recognition of David's favor with God on the part of key figures in Saul's household, Saul stubbornly insisted on making himself David's enemy—and thus God's enemy. At this point, of the three key figures, only Jonathan seemed to have a clear understanding of the full reality regarding David. David was either naive or beginning to become presumptuous that God would always protect him. Saul recognized that God was on David's side—but he was unwilling to accept it. Jonathan's vision was clear. He understood. He got the irony.

Survival on the Boundaries: Ironic Choices

The episode at the big rock concludes the beginning of David's career, his rise to prominence, but the ironic theme of the unreliability of appearance, of the layers of reality, continues throughout David's life. Now a fugitive from the king, reduced to hiding in caves in the southern Judean desert (1 Sam 22), David soon attracted a following of several hundred rascals (1 Sam 22:2) who had to dodge Saul's repeated attempts to capture David and who survived first by eliciting "protection money" from farmers (1 Sam 25). They later pretended to serve Achish, the Philistine (!) king of Gath, as mercenaries (1 Sam 27:1). In exchange, David received Ziklag, a city on the Philistine border with Israel, where Saul would fear to attack. None of these circumstances *seem* like the right choices for a future king of Israel if he wanted to continue to endear himself to the Israelite population. A future king of Israel probably should not have surrounded himself with a band of six hundred failures, debtors, and malcontents (1 Sam 22:2; 23:13), some of them "wicked and base" (1 Sam 30:22), including Hittites (1 Sam 26:6; 2 Sam 11:3), Maachites (2 Sam 23:34; cf. 2 Sam 10:6), and Ammonites (1 Sam 23:37). A future king of Israel probably should not have hidden his parents at the court of the king of Moab, another of Israel's historic rivals (1 Sam 22:3). Apparently, in fact, David's behavior during this period earned him enemies. Doeg, the Edomite (1 Sam 22:9), the people of Keilah (1 Sam

23:12), the Ziphites (twice, 1 Sam 23:19; 1 Sam 26:1), and several unnamed informants (1 Sam 23:25; 24:1) all revealed his whereabouts to King Saul at various times. The people of Ziklag, where David took up residence as a client of King Achish, even threatened to kill him (1 Sam 30:6).

Since the Philistines were Israel's bitter enemies at the time, accepting employment as the head of a mercenary army fighting for Achish seems like a critical error. Whom did Achish expect David to fight against, if not Achich's enemies, the Israelites? In exchange for protection against Saul, Achish surely wanted to see results. How could David ever expect the Israelites to ratify his anointing as king if he had made war on them as a surrogate for the Philistines? That's bad. No, that's good. Evidently, innocent, sweet David had by then learned something about the harsh ways of the world. None of these circumstances *seem* like the proper route to Israel's throne, but we know that this is the story of David's life. Appearance and reality do not always coincide. Indeed, David had learned to utilize the fact that things are not always as they seem to his advantage. Now David himself became the ironist who created the incongruity between appearance and reality.

To satisfy Achish, David made a practice of leading his army on raids against "the Geshurites, the Girzites, and the Amalekites" (1 Sam 27:8), Israel's historical enemies, raids in which he would ruthlessly annihilate entire populations of cities and villages. Returning to Ziklag rich in booty, he would report a successful raid on Israel! In effect and unwittingly, Achish had employed David to fight against Israel's ancient enemies! David skillfully "played both ends against the middle." All the while, his reputation in Israel grew as Achish remained clueless: "Achish trusted David, thinking, 'He has made himself utterly abhorred by his people Israel; therefore he shall be my servant always'" (1 Sam 27:12, NRSV). David even survived the last, very dangerous episode in his "fugitive" period that arose from his entanglement with Achish. When the Philistines decided to band together against Saul and the Israelites, Achish quite naturally included David and his army in the battle preparations, threatening, after all, the ruin of David's ambitions. David could not refuse Achish without revealing his subterfuge; he could not participate in the battle that would eventually cost the lives of both Saul and Jonathan without alienating his fellow Israelites. For a moment, it seemed as though David had outfoxed himself and gotten into a no-win conundrum. "Seemed" is the operative word in irony, however. At the last moment, the other Philistine kings noticed David in the column of advancing troops and insisted that Achish send him back to Ziklag despite Achish's objections that David had "proven" his loyalty. Feigning disappointment, David returned to Ziklag in relief, to await the fateful news from the battlefield that his father- and brother-in-law had both been killed. Achish would soon discover how much the Israelites "utterly abhorred" David. The joke was on Achish!

A review of the ironic character of David's career to this point would emphasize the apparent incongruity evident in the boy singer-shepherd who vanquished a giant, led an army, circumcised Philistines, and escaped a mad king's wrath. It would marvel at the young man's later skill at creating irony—hiring himself out to an enemy king as a mercenary leader only actually to fight against the traditional enemies of his own people and avoiding, at the last moment, disastrous involvement in the decisive battle against Israel and its tragic King Saul. David was never what he seemed—never just the sweet boy, never the potential rival Saul so feared, never loyal to Achish.

A Glimpse of the David to Come

Irony resurfaces in the story of King David some time later in one of the quirkiest episodes in David's life. After successfully eluding Saul until Saul's death, David had now been acclaimed king of all Israel. He realized he needed to consolidate his power. First, he needed a capital city. We know from many sources that, although they were both Israelite and spoke Hebrew, the populations of northern Israel and southern Israel, or Judah, had some rather distinct cultural traditions. For example, they spoke quite distinct dialects, in many ways parallel to the distinction between Southern American English (who call all soda drinks "Co-cola") and the English spoken by Midwesterners (who prefer "pop"). Southerners say "y'all" while Northeasterners say "youse guys." Apparently, David realized that he could potentially create a problem for himself with northerners if he were to select a southern city as his capital; on the other hand, if he were to establish his capital in the North, his fellow southerners would think he was pandering to the North. I have often wondered whether the founding fathers of our country took their cue for creating the District of Columbia from David, because he decided that he needed to establish his capital in a city that was not associated with either the North or the South. At the time, Jerusalem was still under the control of the Jebusites, a native Canaanite group. David simply conquered it with his private army, the mercenaries from the old days in the wilderness, and made it his capital city. Second, David decided that, if he really wanted to bind all twelve tribes together in their loyalty to him, he should also make Jerusalem the center of religion, of worship. To do so, he brought the ark of the covenant there and planned to build a temple before Nathan told him not to do so.

This strategy was apparently entirely David's idea. Scripture records no instruction from the Lord to move the ark. In fact, as they were transporting the ark to Jerusalem in a grand and glorious processional, it toppled, and unfortunate Uzzah put his hand up to steady it. Since he was not a priest, and laypersons were not permitted to touch this most sacred object, unlucky Uzzah fell over dead, bless his heart. David immediately halted the processional.

Apparently he thought, *"Whoa! This could be a sign. It dawns on me now that perhaps I should have asked God's permission to move the ark, after all."* So David went to the nearby home of a certain Obed-Edom and said, *"Look, here's the deal. Now that Uzzah has died this way, I'm not sure whether God approves of my plan to bring the ark to Jerusalem. I would like to leave the ark of the covenant here at your house for a while to see whether any further catastrophes occur as a test of whether my plan pleases God"* (cf. 2 Sam 6:10).

In effect, David must have thought and may have told Obed-Edom, *"If nobody in your household dies, nothing burns down, or anything like that, then I can take that as a positive sign."* Astonishingly, Obed-Edom apparently answered, *"Sure, that'd be fine with me."* He was perfectly willing to play the role of the canary in the coal mine. If someone were to knock on my door and say, "We have this box. Lightning shoots forth from it from time to time when somebody does something with it that you're not supposed to, but we don't know for sure what you are supposed to do and what you aren't supposed to do. We find out we're not supposed to do what we just did when the lightning shoots forth, and by then it's too late. So we wonder whether we can leave it at your house and see if you can figure out the rules for us." My answer would be a definite "No way!" It would not matter if the president of the United States, Moses, and David were asking. Check with the guy across the street.

That's bad? Well, they left the ark with Obed-Edom for a while, and no one died—in fact, Obed-Edom even prospered. So that's good. David concluded that God approved of his plan to move the ark, after all, and that the Uzzah incident must have been a fluke. David resumed the processional, picking up where he had left off. On the last leg of the journey, as the processional approached and entered Jerusalem, the priests and Levites and King David took six steps, lowered the ark to the ground, offered sacrifices, and distributed presents to the crowd. The scene reminds me of Santa Claus at the Macy's Thanksgiving Parade. Next, they distributed raisin cakes to the onlookers (Do you think Little Debbie got the idea from King David?). Then they picked up the ark and took it six more steps. They set it down, they offered sacrifices, they handed out raisin cakes, they picked it up, and so on, until they reached the ark's destination in the city. The final phase of this elaborate procession must have taken the better part of a day. No doubt, it was very expensive. All of Jerusalem must have turned out to witness the grand event.

The most interesting aspect of this episode, which begins the fourth and final phase in David's career, his mature reign, involves the question of the lasting stability of David's kingdom, a question that hinged primarily on the succession. Thus far, Israel has had two kings. Samuel anointed both, but he is dead now. Neither Saul nor David had been obvious choices. The first two kings were not relatives. In fact, Saul had never heard of David until he came to be court musician. It was anyone's guess how the next king would be chosen. Who knows? Some prophet, Elishopar, let us say, may have been out in the countryside right that minute headed to anoint some little boy to be the next king. The last transition between Saul and David had involved Saul's spear-chucking, David's flight to the wilderness, and near civil war. Israel might not have survived another such transfer of power. It was far from a smooth transition. It was nothing like our Inauguration Day when, in a moment, the presidency transfers from one person to another peacefully and in accordance with law and established tradition. Israel had no law governing the transfer of power and no established tradition.

What does the transfer of the ark have to do with the succession to the throne? Nothing is as it seems in the story of David. David had marched the ark into Jerusalem, leading the processional the whole way, dancing at the front of the line. When the celebration was over, "David returned to bless his household." Surely that's good. No, that's bad. "But Michal, the daughter of Saul, came out to meet David and said, 'How the king of Israel honored himself today, uncovering himself today before the eyes of his servants' maids, as any vulgar fellow might shamelessly uncover himself!'" (2 Sam 6:20, NRSV). She was angry. Why?

The Bible says that David wore a linen ephod, something like a military dress uniform in this case. Ancient armies did not wear the typical long robes into battle, because they would have been cumbersome, easy to tangle up in, or easy for an opponent to grab. Instead, ancient warriors basically wore a kilt, a miniskirt (think of the familiar image of the Roman legionnaire; David wore the Israelite equivalent). He was out leaping and dancing—

perhaps the most modest way to put it is to recall that this was in a day before Fruit of the Loom had gone into business. No wonder Michal was mad. *"Just look at you! Out there in front of God and everybody, prancing and dancing the jig, with your skirt flying up. Why, I've never heard of such a shameless display. A fine way for the king to behave!"*

David's response is astonishing. He said to Michal,

> It was before the LORD who chose me in the place of your father [*by the way*] and all of his household to appoint me as prince over Israel and the people of the LORD. [*God chose me, not your family, so there.*] I have danced before the LORD. I will make myself yet more contemptible than this, and I will be abased in my own eyes. [*You haven't seen anything yet, sister.*] (2 Sam 6:21-22a, NRSV)

David's next comment (2 Sam 6:22b) is outrageous, even scandalous: "But by the maids of whom you have spoken, by them I shall be held in honor." What has he said? *"I didn't see any of those young ladies you mention complaining about what they saw! In fact, they seemed to be enjoying themselves."* Advocates of the contemporary liturgical dance movement often appeal to the text, "and David danced before the LORD," as biblical support for dance as an expression of worship. I am an ardent fan of the arts, and I think that anything, including dance, that points to truth, beauty, and goodness can be a way of worshiping God. Still, I think I might consider another scriptural foundation for the practice, because I do not think I recommend that anyone emulate David in detail on Sunday morning at First Baptist Church in your hometown.

Remembering that the point of a good story comes at the end, we should take careful note of the narrator's final comment in verse 23: "And Michal, the daughter of Saul, had no child to the day of her death" (NRSV). What happened here? Michal and David had such a tiff that David apparently sent her to her end of the palace and said, *"Stay down there until I call for you."* What is the significance of the statement that "Michal had no child until the day of her death"? Who would have had a better claim to be the third king of Israel than the grandson of the first king on his mother's side and the son of the second king? Israel has only had two kings; this hypothetical child would have descended directly from both—except that Michal got mad at David for showing his backside, literally. Poor Michal lived a benighted, blighted life: a dowry of Philistine foreskins; a husband on the run from her father; "given" in a second marriage, presumably against her will; divorced from that husband in order to return to David; and now, reduced to virtual widowhood because she did not like it when her husband exposed himself publicly.

A theme other than the difference between appearance and reality that surfaces here runs through the story of David and overlaps with the irony theme, namely, David's many and varied relationships with the women in his life, from the singers who celebrated the boy hero's victory of Goliath down to Abishag the Shunammite at the end of his days. Yet, to have been so "beloved," every indication suggests that he was an abject failure as a husband and as a father: one son died as an infant because of David's adultery and murder; one son, Amnon, raped his half-sister, Tamar; her full brother, Absalom, avenged her humiliation by killing Amnon and then rebelled against his father; a fourth son, Adonijah, attempted a palace coup and was executed by a fifth son, Solomon, the actual successor to David's throne. The Germans have a saying, *Vater werden ist nicht schwer; Vater sein dagegen sehr* (It is not difficult to become a father; being one, on the other hand, is very difficult). The saying applies to many areas of David's life: he became king quickly after Saul's death and consolidated his political power efficiently, but he failed to rule his own household.

Irony to the Very End

In fact, it was the nature of David's relationship with a woman, Abishag, that signaled to everyone at court that David's death was imminent. After working our way through the irony in the story of David up to this point, readers have probably developed the vision to see the ironic humor in this account, i.e., readers should be able to "get it" without assistance, so here is the text. If you do not at least chuckle at the incongruity in this text, then I have failed.

> King David was old and advanced in years, and although they covered him with clothes, he could not get warm. So his servants said to him, "Let a young virgin be sought out for my lord, the king, and let her wait on the king as his attendant. Let her lie in your bosom, so that my lord, the king, may be warm." So they searched for a beautiful girl throughout all the territory of Israel, and found Abishag the Shunammite and brought her to the king. The girl was very beautiful. She became the king's attendant, and served him. But the king did not know her. (1 Kgs 1:1-4, NRSV)

Do you have the picture in your mind? David's advisors staged a Miss Israel contest, and the prize was the opportunity to be the king's hot-water bottle. Ah, it's good to be the king. Many comments come to mind, but my wife or my daughter will probably read this, so I will forgo them. I had a preaching professor once who famously advised his students, "Age takes care of a big part of your sin problem." Apparently, David's womanizing days were over. A diagnosis of David's physical condition might explain why he could not get warm: circulation problems. They put "Miss Israel" in the bed with David and, still, he "could not get warm." As everyone at court seems to have concluded, he must have been nearly dead. The struggle for the throne waged by Adonijah and his supporters, on one hand, and Solomon and his supporters, on the other, began in earnest.

The Theology of Irony

Many forms of humor invite one to recognize the incongruity between what is and what should be. Irony, in contrast, challenges one to discern the incongruity between surface appearance and depth reality, to recognize how something that seems bad can really be good and vice versa. Arguably, then, irony represents the most theological form of humor because it calls for one to look deeply into the obvious for signs of a somewhat veiled but more fundamental truth. Perhaps for this reason, the story of David does not stand alone in the Bible as an example of the challenge of ironic perception. Irony runs through the story of Joseph's life virtually as its overarching theme. On the surface, the course his life took seems stamped by misfortune and betrayal. He was despised by his brothers, sold into slavery, falsely accused, and unjustly imprisoned. Yet, as he came to recognize himself (Gen 45:5-8), beneath and beyond the obvious, God had been at work bringing salvation out of injustice. A paramount sequence of ironies provided Joseph with vital experience as steward of Potiphar's household (as his business manager, as it were), with the opportunity to come to Pharaoh's attention, and, ultimately, with the means to save his family from starvation.

> Bible: Joseph was a prodigy who dreamed of one day leading his family. His father favored him because he was the youngest and, especially, because he was Rachel's son.
> Reader: That's good.
> Bible: No, that's bad because it made his ten older brothers jealous enough to sell him into slavery.
> Reader: That's bad.

Bible: No, that's good because Joseph ended up as the business manager for an Egyptian named Potiphar. Joseph gained a lot of managerial experience.

Reader: That's good.

Bible: No, that's bad because Joseph attracted the attention of Potiphar's wife, who tried to seduce Joseph. When Joseph refused her advances, she accused him of attempted rape. He landed in prison.

Reader: That's bad.

Bible: No, that's good because in prison he came to the attention of two of Pharaoh's officials then out of favor. One of them later suggested that Joseph could interpret Pharaoh's troubling dream about cannibal cows.

Reader: That's good.

Bible: No, that's bad because Joseph said that the dream meant that there would be seven years of famine.

Reader: That's bad.

Bible: No, that's good because Joseph said they would be preceded by seven years of plenty. So Pharaoh put him in charge of storing up during the good years for the bad years to come.

Reader: That's good.

Bible: No, that's bad because Joseph's family was back in Canaan. When the famine came, they faced starvation.

Reader: That's bad.

Bible: No, that's good because Jacob sent some of Joseph's brothers to Egypt to ask for help. After toying with his brothers some, Joseph invited them to bide out the famine with him in Egypt.

Reader: That's good.

Bible: You're dern right that's good.

Similarly, the narrator of the story of Ruth and Naomi observes wryly that Ruth "happened"—"by chance"—to come to glean in the field of Boaz, her deceased husband's apparently wealthy and clearly kind and generous kinsman (Ruth 2:3). God did not openly guide her there, but Naomi (2:20) and the women of Bethlehem (4:14) saw the circumstance as more than an accident.

According to any superficial standard, the execution of Jesus (who had been abandoned by even his closest disciples) represented the failure of an otherwise obscure Palestinian rabbi to found a revolutionary movement in first-century Judaism. That's bad. Seen with the eyes of Easter faith, however, the foundation of the gospel message is the quintessential irony of human history. That's very good indeed. In fact, it is the best!

The test of ironic faith confronts us all every day, in virtually every moment. Is that "just" an oak tree, or does it points beyond itself to a creator? Is my longstanding, rich friendship with Jim "just" an example of normal human interaction, or does it manifest our godlike personhood in caring community? Is your profound love and devotion for your child "just" a biological urge, a primate instinct, or does it grow out of and reflect the love of God for God's children? Do we believe only what we can see objectively, or can we look beyond the sign to the reality? Irony is the substance of faith; it is looking through a glass darkly. It is the joyful laugh of recognition when God brings good out of evil.

Returning to David, we remember God's announcement at the beginning of the story of David's colorful life that things will not be as they seem. Human beings typically want clarity and simplicity. "David was a man after God's own heart." "Peter was the first disciple, the leading apostle." "Paul, the apostle to the Gentiles, was the church's first and greatest missionary." Such statements may be true as far as they go, but they reduce a person such as David to a slogan. David first appears as an innocent, sweet, good-looking kid; by the end of his life, he has become the king of Israel, but also an adulterer and murderer, the father of rebels and rapists, and still one of the most beloved characters in the Bible. Is the story of David's life a tragedy or a comedy? Is it, ironically, both? Good brought out of evil?

The narrator or narrators of David's story do not tell us what we should take away from it. Irony involves a test of perception, in this case, for readers of the Bible. Every reader must make the effort to see through the incongruities of David's life. It seems to me, however, that at least two truths are abundantly clear. First, despite the human tendency to lionize or beatify heroic figures such as David, the Vacation Bible School David is a cartoon character with little resemblance to the biblical David. He was a complex character who lived a complicated life. One could say that, while he may have been "a man after God's own heart," David's own heartbeat was erratic at best. The observation that the David we meet in the Bible was a scoundrel-saint, not the angelic figure of Renaissance art, humanizes him. It does not provide an excuse for misbehavior (*"How can I be expected to live an upright life when even David, 'a man after God's own heart,' sinned so blatantly?"*) but a reminder that every human life is complex and complicated and that every human being faces the challenge of sorting through the detritus of life to find its core, its foundation. If we can learn from David an ironic vision of truth beneath and beyond mere appearance, we may be able to apply that vision to our own lives.

Second, we misread the Bible if we assume that everything reported in it expresses the will of God. Indeed, a central thrust of the David story involves an awareness that, as in the Joseph story or the Jesus story, God may well be at work "behind the scenes," as it were, to influence to the good the outcome of acts that are themselves, in fact, contrary to God's will. Obviously, we can wonder how the story might have gone had Saul taken full account of this truth. When he finally came to the realization that God was at work on David's behalf, he surely must have also realized that his efforts to thwart David's advance were tantamount to efforts to thwart God. God had warned that Saul's kingdom would be given to another; God had not announced Saul's ignominious death in battle. In fact, 1 Samuel 15:24-31 may even suggest that God was willing to forgive Saul for his misdeeds, even though God had decided, firmly, to replace Saul on the throne. Other outcomes were possible if only Saul had translated his insight concerning God's support for David into cooperative action. On the other hand, this awareness that God may be working against the grain of events, so to speak, also cautions against regarding the life of a figure like David, the hero of the story, as a clear model to be emulated. God chose David, but God did not endorse everything that David did. Put simply, David's behaviors are not a biblical warrant for dancing naked in the Christmas pageant, and certainly not for adultery and murder. Irony asks that one distinguish between the false and the true, otherwise one risks becoming the victim of incongruity—that is, becoming the brunt of the joke.

Note

1. D. C. Mueke, *The Compass of Irony* (London: Methuen, 1969) 14; cf. Wayne C. Boot, *A Rhetoric of Irony* (Chicago: University of Chicago, 1974) 10.

Chapter 3

Jonah: A Failure Who Succeeded despite Himself

"What monstrous absurdities and paradoxes have resisted whole batteries of serious arguments, and then crumbled swiftly into dust before the ringing death-knell of a laugh!" (Agnes Repplier)

In many ways, the book of Jonah, one of the twelve so-called Minor Prophets, is unique among the prophets—even odd. First, it is a story. The other prophetic books, both major and minor—Isaiah, Jeremiah, Hosea, Amos, and the others—primarily contain the preaching of the prophets who give the books their names. To be sure, the book of Jonah contains the message that Jonah delivered to the Ninevites, but in Hebrew this message consists of only five words. Five words constitute all the preaching in the book of Jonah. The rest is story. Obviously, one should not read Jonah, then, as one reads the other prophets—that is, with a primary interest in the message conveyed in the prophet's preaching. Instead, one reads Jonah for the message conveyed in the account. It is narrative theology. It communicates meaning and truth in a fashion more comparable to the way a novel or movie communicates meaning and truth than to the way a preacher preaches. In other words, it is important to imagine the events narrated in Jonah on the movie or TV screen in one's mind, paying particular attention to the descriptions, the dialogue, and the plot.

Second, its language is peculiar. The only way to make this peculiarity obvious to a reader of the English Bible is, unfortunately, to play the role of the Hebrew professor. My hope is that linguistics will enhance our appreciation for the humor in the story and not get in the way of doing so. In the introduction, we looked at the fact that humor is closely tied to the possibilities inherent in a given language and talked about how difficult it is to translate puns, plays on words, tone, and rhythm—all important vehicles of humor—from one language into another. I recall seeing a movie during my years in graduate school in Zurich, Switzerland. The Swiss are proud of the fact that most of them speak at least three of the four official Swiss languages, as well as English, so they usually do not dub movies. Instead, they subtitle them in German, French, and Italian. At one point, the lead character in the movie I was watching got into a squabble with detectives and said something like, "Yo' mama," meaning "back off" or "lay off me" in the context. I remember looking down quickly to see how the subtitles would deal with this American street slang. In neither German, French, nor Italian does the phrase "your mother" mean anything other than a reference to one's immediate female ancestor. I nearly choked laughing (the Swiss audience sat silently) because all three subtitles read the equivalent of a polite "Stop, please!" Those translations got the idea but missed the humor. This situation is analogous to the problem we confront in the book of Jonah. Recalling that the essence of humor is the recognition of incongruence, what follows is partly a retelling and partly a simplified language lesson. Thus equipped with the proper lenses for reading the humor in the book of Jonah, here we go.

Act I: Tarshish Bound—Running from God

Without prelude, the book begins with the first, at least apparent, incongruence; it certainly catches one's interest. God charges Jonah with the commission to bear a message to the grand city of Nineveh, the sometimes-capital city of the Assyrian Empire, but God does not specify what the message should be. The Assyrians, one should remember, conquered the northern kingdom of Israel in 722 BCE, taking almost half the population into exile and making the southern kingdom of Judah into a vassal state. They then besieged Jerusalem in 702 BCE, causing mass starvation and humiliating King Hezekiah during the ministry of the prophet Isaiah. Other prophets lambaste Nineveh and the Assyrians for their arrogance with respect to God and their mistreatment of God's people (see, for example, Nahum; Zeph 2:13-15; Isa 10:12; etc.). One might expect that the message God intends for Jonah to deliver will be a message of condemnation similar to Zephaniah's (2:13, my translation): "And he will extend his hand to the north and destroy Assyria, and make Nineveh a desolation, dry as the desert." One might expect such a message, but, incongruously, God says nothing to Jonah about what he should preach to the Ninevites.

The nature of Jonah's mission takes on even greater incongruence, however, through Jonah's entirely ridiculous response. Immediately, by the third verse, the book reports that, instead of setting out for Nineveh as God has instructed him, Jonah "set out to flee to Tarshish from the presence of the LORD." In other words, he headed in the opposite direction, foolishly thinking that by leaving the land of Israel he could escape God's presence! Why was Jonah so unwilling to preach to Nineveh? If he expected, as did Nahum and the others, that God intended to punish Nineveh, he surely would have been eager, even gleeful, to deliver the message of vengeance against such a vicious and hated enemy. Even more foolhardily, however, Jonah seems to think that God is not God in Tarshish (probably modern Spain)! I know that I cannot go to Spain and escape the presence of the God who created Spain. Surely, a prophet of God knew better, too! At the very outset, the narrator alerts readers that something is wrong with Jonah— a prophet who will not preach and who thinks, or behaves as though he thinks, that God's reach does not extend beyond Israel's borders to the Western Mediterranean. Both God's surprising silence regarding the content of Jonah's message to the Ninevites and Jonah's ridiculous attempt to escape God, effectively refusing God's commission, alert readers that, in relation to Jonah's perspective at least, something odd and extraordinary is in the works. Jonah apparently suspects God's motives and intentions. Consequently, the prophet of God seeks to thwart God's plan! Foolhardy, rebellious, comical Jonah.

The story continues to the effect that, in the effort to run away from God, Jonah went down to the port of Joppa and found a ship bound for Tarshish. Throughout the book of Jonah, characteristic features of the Hebrew language function, subtly but significantly, to shape and color the account. At this point, for example, the book reports that Jonah paid "her" fare and boarded "her" with the intention of going "away from the presence of the LORD," as the narrator emphasizes for the second time. Hebrew has no neuter gender, no "it." Every noun must be either masculine or feminine, a circumstance that figures prominently in the storyteller's art in the book of Jonah. Ships are feminine in Hebrew. As will develop in the story, the narrator takes advantage of the fact that all Hebrew nouns have gender to personify inanimate objects and non-personal creatures, much in the same way that fairy tales and children's stories do in English.

The narrator wastes no time on details about the size of the ship, its home port, its name, or its cargo. The story does not linger over the scene, giving no information about the season of the year, the time of day, or the scheduled duration of the journey. Instead, the narrator immediately relates that "the LORD hurled a great wind on the sea, and such a mighty storm came upon the sea that," as the RSV translates it, "the ship threatened to break up" (1:4). Again, the Hebrew takes advantage of the grammatical gender of the word for *ship* here and personifies it. The last phrase in Jonah 1:4 can be translated much more vividly and with greater fidelity to the Hebrew, "the ship thought, 'I am about to be broken up!'" The ship said to herself, *"This is pretty bad; I think I may be in trouble."* The ship itself was afraid, and even the sailors—experienced, tough, rugged, hardened seafaring veterans—were too. They feared for their lives. They began to "hurl" cargo overboard just as God had "hurled" the great wind on the sea, the first indication in the story that this was a commercial vessel, in hopes of easing the strain on the poor ship and preserving themselves. The situation was so dire in their view that they were throwing their merchandise overboard, ending any possibility of profiting from this voyage.

Meanwhile, Jonah, not an experienced sailor and the one individual on board with the most to fear, had gone into the hold of the ship and fallen into a deep sleep! The story uses a form of the same Hebrew word here (*rdm*) that is used to describe Adam's sleep while God made Eve from his rib (*tardemah*, Gen 2:21). The ancient Greek translation says that Jonah was snoring. The ship was afraid, and the sailors were afraid, while Jonah—the cause of the problem—was sound asleep, snoring away as though he had not a care in the world! The captain recognized the incongruity, even though he did not find it at all humorous. "Wake up, sleepy head!" he reprimanded Jonah, calling on him to do the only thing that Jonah, who presumably had no seafaring skills, might conceivably be able to do to save them—pray.

Above decks, since lightening the load had no positive effect, the desperate sailors, suspecting that some deity was angry with someone aboard the vessel, resorted to divination in the effort to get to the bottom of the situation. The lot fell on Jonah, of course. Therefore, the sailors asked him to give an account of himself: "Who are you? What do you do for a living? Where are you from? What is your ethnicity?" Jonah's reply was informative and supremely incongruous: "I am a Hebrew; and I fear the LORD, the God of heaven, who made the sea and the dry land" (1:9, RSV). Astonishingly, Jonah confessed that his God is the God who created the sea and the dry land. We wonder whether Jonah meant to include the dry land over in Spain and the sea that was storming around him even as he spoke. While Jonah made an orthodox confession of faith in the God of Israel, the question is whether he truly believed it. What one truly believes, not just in one's head but also in one's heart—indeed, in one's hands and feet—manifests itself in one's actions more than in one's confessions of faith. How did Jonah plan to escape the presence of the God who made the whole world? Where in the whole world that God made could he go to escape God's presence? To Tarshish? Bless Jonah's heart. Something kept his feet from living out his own confession of faith! He spoke empty words.

When Jonah told the sailors that he was (foolishly) trying to escape the presence of this God who made everything, they only became more afraid (1:10). "The fear of the LORD is the beginning of wisdom" (Prov 1:7). Is it good to be afraid of God? Does God want us to fear him? The word translated "to fear" both here in Jonah and in Proverbs can also be translated "to worship." In fact, just a few verses later, after the storm has been stilled, the book reports that the sailors "feared the LORD greatly, and offered sacrifices, and made vows," that is, they worshiped the God of Israel. In any case, now the sea had grown even more turbulent. The RSV translates, "the sea grew more and more tempestuous" (1:11). The Hebrew personifies again here. It reads, "for the sea was walking and raging," suggesting the image of the pounding waves, like angry footfalls one after the other, smashing into the side of ship. Since, according to his confession, Jonah worshiped the God who made this sea and, moreover, who made it angry because of Jonah's disobedience, the sailors desperately asked Jonah what could be done to avert the impending catastrophe. He should know. His God was causing the storm! Incongruously and calmly, Jonah suggested that the only workable solution was to "hurl" him overboard just as God had "hurled" the wind on the sea and the mariners had "hurled" their cargo into it! Without saying so, Jonah implied that he had no intention of repenting of his course of action. Apparently, this Israelite prophet of God—who could say the catechism with his mouth whether his feet believed it or not—would rather have drowned than comply with God's command to preach to the hated Ninevites.

In yet another incongruity, these heathen sailors, who had moments earlier been praying "each to his god," initially refused to do as Jonah suggested. One might expect that such a group of brazen seafarers would have no compunctions about hurling disobedient Jonah, who had caused them so much trouble, to his deserved fate. At first, however, they chose to try to row back to shore. The Hebrew word translated "to row" can also mean "to plow" or "to dig" and gives the picture of the sailors "digging" hard with their oars as they tried to claw their way to safety. Finally, however, since the sea was still "walking and raging" against them, they turned to their last resort. They prayed to Jonah's God, asking the Lord not to hold against them the blood of this "innocent" man, and "hurled" the troublemaker over the side of the ship like so much flotsam. Immediately, the sea ceased its "walking and raging," and the sailors worshiped the God of Israel, the maker of the sea that had been raging and of the dry land they had so desperately sought to gain. Presumably, the sailors continued their voyage. Their encounter with Jonah cost them their cargo but brought them into relationship with the God of Israel! Not a bad trade.

What of Jonah now? God "appointed" a "big fish" (the Bible does not say "whale") to swallow him. The Hebrew word for "to appoint," which occurs several more times in the story, can also be translated "to ordain." God "ordained" Deacon Fish to the ministry of rescuing Jonah from the depths and transporting him safely back to dry land. Another oddity in the original language has puzzled scholars for generations. The Hebrew word for "fish" used in Jonah 1:17 and 2:1 (*dag*) is masculine. Hebrew can make some masculine nouns feminine by simply adding the suffix -*ah*. Thus, Jonah 2:2 refers to the fish, after it swallowed Jonah, as the *dagah*. In Jonah 2:11, the fish is masculine again. Is the alternation significant, some sort of ancient spelling oddity, or perhaps the equivalent of a typographical error? It is tempting to think of the (male) fish as having temporarily become Jonah's mother, as it were, literally "carrying" Jonah "in his/her belly" safely ashore. In any case, thus ends Act I of Jonah's comedy.

Jonah, a prophet called to go preach to Nineveh, thought that he could go to Tarshish and get away from God. He boarded a merchant marine vessel bound there. No doubt, given the reference to their prayers offered to a variety of gods, the crew constituted a multi-national, multi-ethnic, multi-religious group, as is still true of the merchant marine today. They were not sweet, kind, enlightened gentlemen; they were merchant marines. They were frightened to death while Jonah slept. Jonah would rather have faced death than preach to Ninevites. Yet, inadvertently and incongruously, Jonah ended up converting the sailors, who, contrary to all expectations, appear to be the heroes of Act I. Jonah evangelized them by means of the testimony of his stubborn disobedience. Remarkably, they learned to fear God. Did Jonah?

Interlude: Jonah Prays a Pious Prayer

The prayer that Jonah prayed from the belly of the great fish would seem in some ways to suggest that he had learned to fear God. The RSV translates it as follows:

> I called to the LORD, out of my distress, and he answered me;
> out of the belly of Sheol I cried, and thou didst hear my voice.

For thou didst cast me into the deep, into the heart of the seas,
and the flood was round about me; all thy waves and thy billows passed
over me.
Then I said, "I am cast out from thy presence;
how shall I again look upon thy holy temple?"
The waters closed in over me, the deep was round about me;
weeds were wrapped about my head at the roots of the mountains.
I went down to the land whose bars closed upon me for ever;
yet thou didst bring up my life from the Pit, O LORD my God.
When my soul fainted within me, I remembered the LORD;
and my prayer came to thee, into thy holy temple.
Those who pay regard to vain idols forsake their true loyalty.
But I with the voice of thanksgiving will sacrifice to thee;
what I have vowed I will pay. Deliverance belongs to the LORD! (2:2-9)

Jonah certainly used all the right words, the irony of his claims that
God (!) cast him into the sea and that he has been "cast from [God's] presence" notwithstanding. In fact, of course, he had actively been running from
God—any supposed separation from God was his own doing. The mariners
"hurled" him into the sea, not God, and they did so only because Jonah
himself insisted on it rather than join in their prayers of repentance! Besides,
God made that very sea, ruled it, and ordained one of its creatures to preserve Jonah's life, despite his disobedience! Similarly, the contrast he drew
between himself and idol worshipers (like the sailors who came to fear God
and the Ninevites who would later repent) and the complete absence of any
note of repentance or penitence also stand out. Still, commentators note
that Jonah speaks of deliverance from his predicament as though it had
already taken place and vows a sacrifice of thanksgiving when he makes it
back to the temple to worship. Did Jonah thereby express confident faith
in God's mercy and power to save? Is his prayer evidence of a new appreciation for the fact that God gives second chances? Or could this prayer simply
be another example of Jonah's tendency to make pious pronouncements of
orthodox faith whether sincere or not? Jonah's behavior in the two acts of
the comedy that follow will tell the tale.

Act II: Let's Try this Again

The action resumes in Act II with the "big fish" delivering, literally "spewing" or "vomiting," Jonah onto the dry land (2:11 [Eng 2:10]) at God's
command. A college friend used to say that Jonah must have given the fish
indigestion and that "spewing onto the dry land" was "Bible talk" for getting

the dry heaves. In any case, God now reset circumstances to give Jonah a second chance to carry out God's commission. After the opening comment that "the word of the LORD came to Jonah a *second time* [emphasis added], saying . . . ," Jonah 3:2 repeats 1:2 almost verbatim. In response this time, however, Jonah actually set out for the great city of Nineveh. The text emphasizes Nineveh's grandeur by commenting that it is "a journey of three days" (3:3). We do not know how to take this comment, except that it seems to be hyperbole. Theoretically, it could mean that Jonah had a journey of three days ahead of him before he reached Nineveh, but there is no sea coast within three days of Nineveh using ancient methods of transportation. It must, therefore, describe Nineveh's size, in which case, it would mean that Nineveh was a three-day journey either in circumference or in diameter. A city of such size would rival, if not surpass, modern cities such as New York, Tokyo, or Paris. Ancient Nineveh was not so grand, but it must have seemed so to the author of the Jonah story.

In any case, Jonah made a day's journey toward the center of the city, stopped, and *finally* delivered his rather unusual message. It stands out for three reasons. First, Jonah's sermon is exceptionally brief, only five words in Hebrew—so brief, in fact, that it is difficult to translate into English with the same economy of words. Second, since it is so brief, it represents perhaps the most incomplete sermon ever preached. Normally, prophetic judgment preaching describes the wrong being done, advocates an alternative pattern of behavior, warns of potential consequences of continuing in sin, calls for repentance, and, above all else, does so in God's name. Apparently, while Jonah had decided that he must fulfill God's commission to preach to Nineveh, he was determined to meet only the bare minimal requirement—the letter of God's call, not the spirit of it. God said to preach to Nineveh; God did not say what to preach. With five words, Jonah obeyed—technically. Why was Jonah so determined to obstruct God's will? Third, Jonah's sermon proves to be oddly ambiguous. That is, in the end, it meant almost the opposite of what Jonah intended. Jonah (or God?) chose as the key verb a word with the basic meaning "to turn" or "to change," which often means "to be overturned, destroyed" (in Gen 19:21, 25, 29, it refers to the destruction of Sodom and Gomorrah, surely Jonah's hope for Nineveh) but can also mean "to change," sometimes approximating the sense of "to repent" (cf. Hos 11:8). An awkward but serviceable English translation that preserves the ambiguity might be, "Within forty days, Nineveh turns!" or "You have forty more days!"

This is simply a brilliant sermon, is it not? It is grand rhetoric, moving, picturesque, detailed, theologically profound, full of human compassion and divine challenge, is it not?

No, it is not. It is the sorriest sermon in the Bible. Forty days until what, exactly? What were the Ninevites to do during those forty days? Should they be afraid or hopeful, resigned to their fate or motivated to repentance? What did they need to change? Who wanted them to change? On whose authority did Jonah make this proclamation? Assuming that it is an exhortation to change, to whom were the Ninevites to pray and of what were they to repent? Jonah did not even mention God! He spoke these five words and left. This is not good preaching by any standard! Apparently, Jonah had decided that if God was going to insist that he preach to Nineveh, he would go through the motions, but he would try to ensure that his preaching made no difference whatsoever!

The great prophets Hosea, Isaiah, Jeremiah, and Ezekiel had lengthy ministries of preaching to God's chosen people, yet their powerful and eloquent messages went largely unheeded. We might well expect that, as Jonah apparently hoped, Jonah's pitiful five words to the pagan Ninevites would have no impact. Incongruously, however,

> The people of Nineveh believed God and they proclaimed a fast and they put on sackcloth, from the greatest to the least of them. When the word reached the king of Nineveh, he arose from his throne, removed his robe, put on sackcloth, and sat on the ash heap. Then he declared, saying, "In Nineveh, by decree of the king and his nobles: Human beings and beasts, cattle and flocks are not to even taste anything or to graze and they are not to even drink water. Human beings and animals are to put on sackcloth and they are to cry mightily out to God, turn each and everyone from their evil ways and from the violence in their hands. Who knows, perhaps God will turn and relent and his anger may turn aside so that we do not perish?" (3:5-9, my translation)

It is important to note certain almost absurd details of this Ninevite reaction to Jonah's preaching. First, spontaneously, without hesitation, and with no guidance from Jonah or the priests or rulers of Nineveh, these pagan Assyrians whom Jonah so despised—and whom readers of Jonah, if they knew the history of relations between Assyria and Israel, also likely despised—began fasting and lamenting in typical expressions of repentance and penitence in Israel and Assyria in that time. Second, when the king heard of Jonah's sermon, he not only began fasting and lamenting himself but also issued the redundant and ridiculously incongruous decree that all the people of Nineveh *and all the livestock*—all the cows and sheep and goats—were not even to taste food (or graze, in the case of the animals). Further, they were to abstain even from drinking water, to dress in sackcloth, the clothing of the mourner and the penitent, to pray "mightily" to God, and to reform their behaviors. The image of cows fasting, clad in sackcloth, sitting on the ash heap, repenting, and praying to God is the very definition of absurd comic incongruity. From cow to king, the Ninevites had a prayer meeting! We should remember the image well because it becomes important at the conclusion of the story. Third, the king's rationale for this human and animal penitence—"Who knows, perhaps God will turn and relent and his anger may turn aside so that we do not perish?" (3:9)—suggests that the Assyrian king was a better theologian than the Israelite prophet Jonah! Apparently, the Assyrian king chose to interpret Jonah's ambiguous sermon about things "turning" in Nineveh as a reference to repentance that might, in fact, motivate God to "turn" away from God's intention to punish. The result? "When God saw their actions, that they had turned from their evil ways, God relented of the calamity that God announced, and did not do it" (3:10). Fourth, and finally, for the second time in the account, Jonah had inadvertently—against his will and contrary to his intention— evangelized people he despised.

Act III: Jonah Does Not Like What He Knows about God

One might expect that the story would end here. God commissioned Jonah to preach to the Ninevites. After a false start, Jonah fulfilled the commission, at least nominally. Almost miraculously, certainly incongruously, Jonah's message hit home: the Ninevites repented, God forgave them, and everyone lived happily ever after. Well, not everyone. The Hebrew of Jonah 4:1 is colorful. A "literal" translation would be awkward and ungrammatical English. In order to convey the tone, one could paraphrase it something like, "And, for Jonah, this was a very disastrous outcome; it made him hot under the collar."

We do not have to wait long for the story to tell us why Jonah did not want to go to Nineveh in the first place, why, when he finally acquiesced, he preached the sorriest sermon ever, and why he was now so angry. Ultimately, Jonah was angry with God for being merciful. In his prayer to God, he explained that the reason he had tried to run off to Tarshish in the first place was because he had been afraid that God would do something like this. He did not admit, but we can suspect, that the reason he had preached such a short, enigmatic, downright inadequate sermon was in an attempt to *avoid* persuading the Ninevites to repent. He seems to have tried to fulfill God's commission technically, but he did not give a whole-hearted effort. Still, and despite himself, *it worked*, just as he had feared!

The Hebrew is colorful here, too. Literally, Jonah blamed God for being a God "of grace and mercy, and with a long nose" (4:2). The Hebrew idiom usually translated "to become angry" is, literally, "to become hot of nose." Hebrew associates the emotion of anger with one of its physical manifestations—the flared nostril, the flush of adrenalin. (Incidentally, if the ancient Hebrews had been much like me, the expression might have been "hot of ears." When I become angry, my ears become hot and turn red. I may be sitting quietly, but if my ears have reddened, I am angry, even if I am controlling it.) In turn, Hebrew describes someone who is patient and slow to anger as "long of nose," that is, as someone whose nose does not become red hot quickly. In effect, Jonah told God, *"I know you; I know you have a slow nose, that you do not have a quick temper. You are just the kind of God who forgives sinners. You do that kind of stuff all the time. The whole reason I ran and then eventually preached a sorry sermon was to avoid this. Now, look what you have done! You have forgiven Assyrians, of all people!"*

Jonah culminated his complaint with the request that God simply let him die. Once before, he had demonstrated that he would rather die than preach to the Ninevites. Now that he had preached to them, they had repented, and God had forgiven them, he found that he could not bear the idea that his preaching had resulted in salvation for Assyrians! *"I tried to drown, but you would not let me."* God responded with another question, "Does your anger do you any good?" (4:4, literally, "Does it do any good that it burns you?").

"Then Jonah left the city and sat down east of the city. He made himself a shelter and sat under it in the shade, waiting to see what would happen in the city" (4:5, my translation). Jonah may have hoped that before the forty days transpired, the Assyrians might backslide and God would return to the original intention of punishing their evil. In Jonah's mind, they were awful pagans, after all. Now the reason that the story does not end with the repentance of the Assyrians begins to emerge. The sailors had repented. The Ninevites had repented. Only one figure remained unrepentant. Apparently, the God who was willing to forgive sailors and Ninevites was not yet ready to give up on Jonah. Just as he learned by experience the truth of his confession that God made sea and dry land, Jonah now needed to learn by experience the truth of the confession concerning God's grace, mercy, and patience. God's peculiar way of teaching this lesson, however, matched Jonah's absurdity.

The story continues with the report that "the LORD God ordained a bush and it grew up over Jonah to shade his head to save him from his discomfort" (4:6, my translation). Deacon Bush joins the fearful ship, Reverend Fish, and the penitent cows, goats, and sheep in the cast of non-human characters in the story of Jonah. Incidentally, no one knows what kind of plant the Hebrew word *qiyqayon* denotes. Scholars have speculated as to what species of plant could have grown overnight to sufficient stature to shade Jonah from the sun. Some have suggested a variety of gourd. No one knows for sure. In any case, Jonah was delighted by the relief from the blazing sun, but not for long. As the next day dawned, God ordained a worm (Bishop Worm, meet Deacon Bush)—probably a cutworm, though again, we do not know. The text says that Bishop Worm "smote" the plant, and it withered. By the time the sun had fully risen, God had ordained a "sultry" east wind to blow on Jonah, now bereft of his shade plant. God sent quite a contingent to minister to Jonah—Reverend Fish, Deacon Bush, Bishop Worm, and now Brother Wind. Brother Wind beat down all day on Jonah, who was sitting exposed to the full sun. Coming from the east, off the desert, this wind was hot, dry, and relentless. Such winds are called *siroccos* today. Jonah sat on the hillside waiting in vain to see Nineveh's destruction. The sun beat down on him and the wind assaulted him. The sun and the wind, the wind and the sun. Finally, frustrated with God and suffering physically, Jonah lamented, "It would be better for me to die than to live."

The story draws to its conclusion—the punch line. Remembering that in all narrative art, especially in humor, the climax occurs at the end, we want to pay particular attention. Everything has been set up. We have gotten to know Jonah rather well as a petulant, prejudiced, prideful preacher of pitiful prophecy. Among the prophets of ancient Israel, Jonah has no equal. He could say the right things about God creating the whole world, both the sea and dry land, but he did not seem to truly believe them. Worse, he knew that God is merciful and gracious, but *he did not want this to be true*—at least not for everyone! One would think that a prophet of Israel would celebrate God's willingness, even eagerness, to forgive. Jonah probably should have recognized that he, too, needed God's forgiveness. Instead, he would rather have died than continue in the service of a God who would forgive Assyrians. (Do you get mad at God because God readily and quickly forgives your enemies or people you do not think deserve forgiveness?)

Now, the punch line, as it were, comes in a dialogue between God and Jonah that ends the book and gives God the last word. The morning after Reverend Worm ate Deacon Bush, God started the discussion by asking a question: "Is your anger over the bush doing you any good?" Jonah responded, "My anger to death is, indeed, doing me good" (4:9, my translation). In effect, Jonah answered, *"You bet it is doing me good. I am so angry I could just die, which is what I would rather do than sit here in the hot wind under the hot sun and watch those horrible Ninevites go on about their lives because you forgave them. You took away my shade and forgave my enemies. Let me die and be done with Ninevites and the heat and with you, too, for that matter."*

God's response, a rhetorical question in two parts that establishes an analogy between Jonah and God, ends the discussion and the book (4:10-11). The first part of the question focuses on Jonah's personal investment in the plant that had shaded him briefly from the heat of the desert sun: *"You are all worked up over the plant, even though you had nothing to do with it growing up where and when it did in the first place and even though it is just a plant, after all, with little more life expectancy under the best conditions than the day and night it actually lived."*

The second part contrasts Jonah's selfish reaction to the death of an impersonal plant with God's investment in the Ninevites. *"Yet you do not want me to get worked up over Nineveh, where more than 120,000 people live?"* The implication is, of course, that God did in fact create and nurture the Ninevites; they are human beings whom God made in God's image as surely as God made, called, and spared Jonah, the Israelite prophet—who, after all, had been as disobedient as the Ninevites, if not more so. If God were not the kind of God who forgives Ninevites, God would not be the kind of God to forgive Jonah either.

Satirical Theology for a Cynical Age?

"Besides," God said, "there are many cows there." They repented too, remember. A ship deliberated over its own destruction. A fish pregnant with a wayward prophet transported the prophet safely back to shore. Ordained winds, ordained fish, ordained plants, and ordained worms. Repenting cows. I remember well the first time I read this book in Hebrew as a seminary student. I was preparing for class the next day, and when I got to "and besides that, many cows" (4:11), I was convinced that I had not gotten it right and hoped that the professor would not call on me to translate that passage the next day. I could not imagine a book of the Bible ending with God's insinuation that God may have spared Nineveh for the sake of repentant cows! Of course, the professor called on me. I read. He said, "That's right." I said, "But what does it mean?" He said, "You tell me."

In the meantime, I have come to understand the whole book of Jonah in relation to the cows. God drove home the point that Jonah's anger was useless and selfish. Jonah may have been able to say the right things about God, but he sometimes acted as though he did not believe them, and sometimes he did not like that what he said about God was true. He did not want God to be God everywhere. He did not want God to forgive just any of God's children who repented. In short, Jonah wanted God to do things Jonah's way. Someone in this story looks even more foolish than cows at a prayer meeting! A prophet of Israel could confess that Israel's God made the entire universe, sea and sand alike, but imagined that he could elude God by going to Tarshish! A prophet who did not want to preach! A prophet who did not want to see people repent! A prophet who, in the effort to get himself killed, accidentally converted crusty sailors and, by means of the sorriest sermon recorded in Scripture, converted cows and even, despite himself, the very Ninevites he had hoped to see destroyed!

Humor points out incongruities; it tells the truth. The point of the story of Jonah is not in the message he preaches but in the pitiful, laughable incongruities of his life—and of ours. Too often, we also foolishly think that we can elude God; too often, we also ridiculously divide the world into those whom God favors (of course, they are usually people like ourselves) and those who do not merit God's mercy. Pitifully, foolishly, foolhardily, we want God to adhere to our expectations; we want our enemies to be God's enemies; we want God to shade us from the discomfort of the bright sun while we gloat as God destroys those we hate. But God loves the cows, too.

Too often, our words say the right things about God, but our behaviors betray our insincerity or, worse, our distaste for God's way of doing things—caring for cows and loving our enemies. God's closing question to Jonah, like Jonah's confession of faith to the sailors, calls to mind the biblical doctrine of creation and two of its central assertions, namely (1) that God regards all the living things God created as "good" and (2) that God created human beings—all of us—in God's image. Jonah's attitude, in contrast, seems anachronistically contemporary. For him, plants mattered only because they gave him shade. He certainly did not care that the cows repented. He saw himself as the center. He was certainly no ecologist;

instead, he was a bigot of the worst kind. He knew in his head that God cared about Assyrians, but he did not like it. In Jonah's view, his enemies should also be God's enemies—forever and ever, amen!

Do you see any resemblance between Jonah and contemporary Christians? Do we think we can hide from God by napping deep down in the holds of our offices Monday through Friday? Do we make pious confession with our mouths while our feet run to Tarshish, away from God's call on our lives? Do we try to satisfy God's call with minimal compliance by attending an occasional Sunday service? Do we dislike the idea that God loves our worst enemy as much as God loves us? God bless America (and hang the rest of the world?)! The God of the book of Jonah pities cows. Do we value God's good creation only for the shade it can offer us from the blazing sun? Jonah was an incongruous buffoon, a prophet of God who did not want to preach because he did not like the fact that God forgives even Assyrians. We may be just as ridiculous as Jonah was, no matter what we profess to believe. Satire comically tells the painful truth.

Chapter 4

Esther: The Cocktail Party Queen

"Against the assault of laughter nothing can stand."
(Mark Twain)

"Comedy is defiance. It's a snort of contempt in the face
of fear and anxiety. And it's the laughter that allows hope
to creep back on the inhale." (Will Durst)

We find humor in individual stories throughout the Bible, in Genesis or
episodes in the life of King David, for example. The book of Esther may be
the only book in the Bible, however, that can be classified, start to finish, as
a comedy. Esther represents a puzzle that has troubled biblical scholarship
for centuries. Only since scholars have begun to deal with the possibility of
humor in the Bible have they suggested that the solution to the puzzle of
Esther may lie in the fact that the book belongs to a comic genre. What is
this puzzle that daunted scholarship for so long? It is the problem of history,
a problem that culminates in the troubling violence at the end of the book
and that is compounded by the fact that this biblical book does not mention
God—not once.

Historical "Fact" and Comical Truth

The Bible is not a book; it is a collection of books. Each book in the Bible
belongs to a genre of some kind: Gospels, history, letters, legal collections,
poetry and prayers, proverbial wisdom, etc. When we call the Bible the word
of God, we are talking about how it speaks to us; we are not talking about
a genre. Therefore, as with any other book of the Bible, if one wishes to read
Esther properly, one of the first questions to ask concerns its specific genre.
One reads the phone book differently than one reads a Shakespearean son-
net, for example. Obviously, the rules for interpreting a science textbook
differ from those for interpreting a science-fiction novel. By the same token,

one can expect a different set of dynamics to be at work in the biblical psalms of lament than in the Beatitudes. Moreover, nothing on the face of Scriptures suggests that there are genres that should not appear in the Bible. Indeed, the Bible even contains fiction. Jesus told fictional parables. With regard to literature, fiction is not the opposite of fact. There is truth in fiction. We can hear the word of God in a fictional account.

On its face, the book of Esther seems to fall into the genre category of history; on closer examination, however, virtually no figure and no event recorded in it appear to be "historical." The first figure encountered in the book of Esther, King Ahasuerus of Persia, already raises the problem. While the ancient Assyrians were ruthless conquerors, the Babylonians efficiently exploited the territories they controlled, the Greeks spread their philosophy and aesthetics throughout the Mediterranean world, and the Romans engineered and legislated. In contrast, the Persians were bureaucrats. Their administrative structures kept accurate and copious records. While historians debate details in the succession of Persian kings, they know the names of these kings, just as historians can also identify the Persian queens and the Persian prime ministers. Yet Persian sources do not record a King Ahasuerus. Therefore, many English Bibles identify the Persian king in the book of Esther as one of the known Persian kings, "Artaxerxes," the name already found in the Greek Septuagint of the Old Testament. The translators of the Greek Septuagint apparently recognized that there had been no Ahasuerus, but there had been several kings named Artaxerxes. Since both names begin with an "a" sound and end in an "s" sound, the translators seem to have concluded that "Ahasuerus" must really mean "Artaxerxes"—a pretty big logical leap.

The ancient Greek translators' assumption can be tested. Did Artaxerxes have a queen named Vashti, the name of Ahasuerus's queen according to the book of Esther? According to the Persian sources, no. Nor were there any Persian queens named Vashti or Esther/Hadassah. The Persian records do not mention prime ministers named Haman or Mordecai. They know nothing of decrees permitting the annihilation of the Jews or permitting the Jews to take preemptive measures to counteract the earlier decree. In fact, none of the figures who appear in the book of Esther and none of the events recorded there can be identified in the Persian sources. Scholars cannot find reference in Persian historical sources to a single moment, event, person, circumstance, or setting narrated in Esther, and they have tried mightily to do so. Now, if one were dealing with an "Under-secretary of State for Israelite Affairs," say, one might not be troubled not to find reference to him by name in the Persian records, but when one king, two queens, and two prime ministers are missing from the historical records, one must account for the situation.

Recent scholarship on Esther has begun to explore the possibility that Esther exemplifies the specific genre of comic literature known as farce and that, therefore, Esther was never, in fact, meant to be a historical book. Farcical literature overdraws its subject in order to point out how ridiculous it is. The long-running television variety show *Saturday Night Live* deals heavily in farce, especially in their famed opening sequences in which they often reenact events from contemporary political life. All of the presidents of the United States who have held office since SNL went on the air in the late 1970s have been the subject of such farcical exposure. In fact, SNL often makes powerful people like presidents of the United States look downright idiotic. In doing so, the show fulfills an important social function. The powerful do behave idiotically sometimes, and the fact needs to be pointed out so that the powerful and everyone else do not forget that even presidents are human beings with human foibles.

Even in the ancient period, when the Greeks wrote about the Persians, they commented on how bureaucratic the Persian government was, on how ornate Persian clothing, furnishings, and architecture were, and on how pompous the Persians themselves were. A good analogy for the Persians from more recent history would be the French in the period of Louis XVI, the period that led up to the French Revolution—a society lampooned in the farcical Mel Brooks film *The History of the World, Part I*. If one wanted to target the Persians for ridicule, then, one would likely exaggerate, to the point of absurdity, their fascination with administrative structures, forms, rules, regulations, record keeping, and so forth, as well as their lavish lifestyle. Does the book of Esther exhibit the characteristics of farce? Can one attribute the lack of a specific historical connection to the fact that the author or authors of Esther, who would have been Jews living under Persian (or perhaps Greek) domination, wanted to ridicule the empire but also wanted to stay out of jail?

In fact, almost every feature of the book of Esther is outlandishly overblown and intricate. The plot of Esther, in many ways comparable to the plots of Shakespearean comedies, involves a mainline of the story augmented and interrupted by a number of subplots ("Meanwhile, back in the palace . . ."). Sometimes, a subplot seems at first unrelated to the overall story, but it later rejoins the main sequence of events so that, in the end, everything links together and culminates in a grand resolution. In sum,

Esther exhibits every mark that it is intentional, intricate, intensely satirical *farce*.

Hyperbole and Ridicule

The book begins with farcical hyperbole. Apparently, the events related in the book of Esther happened "in the days of Ahasuerus, the Ahasuerus who reigned from India to Ethiopia over one hundred and twenty-seven provinces" (Esth 1:1, RSV). One hundred twenty-seven? From India to Ethiopia? Was that, in fact, the extent of the Persian Empire? At times, it reached as far as the northern border of India and included "Cush," as the Bible refers to Ethiopia. Were there, in fact, one hundred twenty-seven provinces? Not quite. The so-called Behistun Inscription (1.6) of Darius lists twenty-three (one hundred and four short): "Persia, Susiana, Babylonia, Assyria, Arabia, Egypt, the (lands) which are on the sea, Sparda, Ionia, [Media], Armenia, Cappadocia, Parthia, Drangiana, Aria, Chorasmia, Bactria, Sogdiana, Ga(n)dara, Scythia, Sattagydia, Arachosia, [and] Maka."

Esther's hyperbole continues:

> In those days when King Ahasuerus sat on his royal throne in Susa the capital, in the third year of his reign he gave a banquet for all his princes and servants, the army chiefs of Persia and Media and the nobles and governors of the provinces being before him, while he showed the riches of his royal glory and the splendor and pomp of his majesty for many days, a hundred and eighty days.
>
> And when these days were completed, the king gave for all the people present in Susa the capital, both great and small, a banquet lasting for seven days, in the court of the garden of the king's palace. There were white cotton curtains and blue hangings caught up with cords of fine linen and purple to silver rings and marble pillars, and also couches of gold and silver on a mosaic pavement of porphyry, marble, mother-of-pearl and precious stones. Drinks were served in golden goblets, goblets of different kinds, and the royal wine was lavished according to the bounty of the king. And drinking was according to the law, without constraint; for the king had given orders to all the officials of his palace to do as every man desired. Queen Vashti also gave a banquet for the women in the palace which belonged to King Ahasuerus. (Esth 1:2-9, RSV)

The book of Esther depicts a scenario here that is outrageous beyond all imagination. First, I want to take issue with a common English translation of one of the key terms in this passage, the Hebrew termed rendered "banquet" in the RSV and most other English versions of the Bible, because it is inaccurate and impedes an understanding of the story. The Hebrew word is *mishteh*. In Hebrew, one way to make a noun from a verb is to prefix an "m." Similarly, in English, one can make a noun of a verb by suffixing the syllable "er" to denote someone who or something that performs the action of the verb. For example, someone who bakes is a baker; something that sprinkles is a sprinkler. The Hebrew prefix can denote someone or something that performs the action of the verb, it can denote the action performed, or it can refer to the place where the action occurs. In this case, the Hebrew verb is *shatah*, "to drink," so a *mishteh* is a "drinking." People *eat* at banquets. In fact, the image that the word "banquet" brings to mind is of a large hall with well-appointed tables, probably a head table for the host and any dignitaries or honored guests, fine food, and a wait staff in attendance. It is an orderly affair focused around the meal, conversations at table, and perhaps a speech or some other formal presentation. The word *mishteh* derives etymologically from a word for drinking, not from a word for eating. Why do translators fear rendering it more appropriately?

Someone may object that this interpretation bases too much on etymology, but the gatherings described in Esther were clearly not banquets. Instead, the festivities mentioned in Esther were obviously *drinking parties.* In fact, the text goes to great lengths to describe the events as such. The decorations were lavish; partygoers could choose from a wide variety of golden flagons; the king's wine flowed like an everlasting stream. Moreover, the king had issued specific orders apparently designed to ensure that the party was lively: "Drinking was by flagons, without restraint" (1:8, NRSV). The king had given orders that there was to be no sipping; "No restrictions!" (1:8, TNK; or as the NIV translates more demurely, "By the king's command each guest was allowed to drink in his own way"). Even King Ahasuerus himself became "merry with wine" (v. 10), merry enough, in fact, to cause trouble with his missus—more on that later. Thus, these celebrations were not *banquets.* In contemporary parlance, one might describe them, depending on the level of society involved, as cocktail parties or even as "keggers."

Ahasuerus threw a 180-day, or six-month-long, cocktail party (talk about binge drinking!). The guests consisted of virtually the entire government: the royal family and the officials of the court (the ancient equivalent of the president's cabinet), the joint chiefs of the Persian military, and the governors of all the provinces. The governor of India had come all the way to Susa, the capital city of Persia, to drink with all the other governors for six months. After the 180-day drinking party for the leadership, Ahasuerus apparently thought more celebration was in order, so he pitched a weeklong affair for the citizenry of Susa. Perhaps Andrew Jackson, who opened the White House to the public at his inauguration, got the idea from Ahasuerus. Esther does not tell us, however, that the drunken citizens of Susa trashed the palace, as the Washingtonians did Jackson's White House. Who was running the government, meanwhile? If, rather than hyperbole and satire, this account is taken as a historical report, it defies explanation. These 187 days (how long would the hangover from such a party have persisted?) would have been the ideal time, say, *to attack Persia*. Surely the Greeks, Persia's sworn enemies, would have heard that the entire Persian government, including its leading generals, was on a six-month drunk! Surely they would have exploited the weakness. Surely no king, Persian or otherwise, would be so foolhardy as to risk such an attack. We criticize our presidents for taking a week of vacation; we would impeach them for such foolhardiness, waste, and frivolity.

Making Room for the Heroes of the Story: Trouble at Home for the King

The book takes another tack, however. The king's drunkenness made him vulnerable not internationally, but domestically. He got into trouble with his wife! On the seventh day of the second *mishteh*, or the 187th day since he had begun his marathon cocktail party, the king commanded his seven chief servants "to bring Queen Vashti before the king with her royal crown, in order to show the peoples and the princes her beauty; for she was fair to behold. But Queen Vashti refused to come at the king's command conveyed by the eunuchs. At this the king was enraged, and his anger burned within him" (1:11-12, RSV).

Again the book of Esther presents interpreters with a puzzle. Why would the king decide, in a moment of drunkenness, to parade his queen before an audience as though she were a prize horse? Had they never seen the queen before? Why would the queen refuse the king? Is something sinister lurking beneath the surface here? Does this episode reflect some Persian custom or cultural expectation, unknown to us, that would explain the interpersonal dynamics at play? Scholarly efforts to take Esther as historical literature have run aground on these questions. Again, however, taking clues from the fact that the figures we meet in Esther do not seem to be historical personages and from the ludicrous image of the Persian king on a 187-day binge, the problem fades away if one assumes this episode to be satire, too. What does it satirize, then? The text answers this question for us.

Then the king consulted the sages who knew the laws (for this was the king's procedure toward all who were versed in law and custom, and those next to him were Carshena, Shethar, Admatha, Tarshish, Meres, Marsena, and Memucan, the seven officials of Persia and Media, who had access to the king, and sat first in the kingdom):

"According to the law, what is to be done to Queen Vashti because she has not performed the command of King Ahasuerus conveyed by the eunuchs?"

Then Memucan said in the presence of the king and the officials, "Not only has Queen Vashti done wrong to the king, but also to all the officials and all the peoples who are in all the provinces of King Ahasuerus. For this deed of the queen will be made known to all women, causing them to look with contempt on their husbands, since they will say, 'King Ahasuerus commanded Queen Vashti to be brought before him, and she did not come.' This very day the noble ladies of Persia and Media who have heard of the queen's behavior will rebel against the king's officials, and there will be no end of contempt and wrath! If it pleases the king, let a royal order go out from him, and let it be written among the laws of the Persians and the Medes so that it may not be altered, that Vashti is never again to come before King Ahasuerus; and let the king give her royal position to another who is better than she. So when the decree made by the king is proclaimed throughout all his kingdom, vast as it is, all women will give honor to their husbands, high and low alike."

This advice pleased the king and the officials, and the king did as Memucan proposed; he sent letters to all the royal provinces, to every province in its own script and to every people in its own language, declaring that every man should be master in his own house. (1:13-22, NRSV)

At this point, readers may smile or shake their heads. The Persian court was in turmoil. It faced a constitutional crisis because the queen would not answer the king's pointless summons to put herself on public display. The king asked what the law said about disobedient wives and learned that, apparently, Vashti's refusal to obey the king was unprecedented. His counselors responded, in effect, *We have never had a wife tell her husband 'no' before! Especially not a queen. This sets a bad precedent. You'd better make a law!* Accordingly, the emperor issued a law requiring husbands throughout the empire to "man up" and be the boss in their own homes. Can this possibly have been serious politics and reasonable governmental policy, or do all the clues indicate that this is a ridiculous proposition meant to satirize Persian bureaucracy? The myth of the husband as the lord of his castle may well have its roots right here. Largely because of this part of the story, some think that a woman wrote the book of Esther. It now directs its satire not just at Persian emperors but also at lesser tyrants—Persian (and probably also Jewish) husbands.

Throughout Scripture and contemporary experience, the myth of the husband as lord of his castle competes with the folksy truism, "If mama ain't happy, ain't nobody happy." The notion that a law can establish the propriety of unequal power relations in a marriage is laughable. Even the grand Persian Empire cannot enact a law with the power to contravene the laws of nature. Ask Abraham whether he would have wanted to contradict Sarah when she had her mind made up. Ask Isaac whether he ever successfully resisted Rebekah's determination. Ask Jacob what it was like to come home from work at the end of the day to find that his wives had been haggling and bargaining over who had the right to him for the evening and that he had no say in the matter. I sometimes remark that my wife is the most submissive woman in human history. When we married, I told her that on most matters, she should do as she pleases, and that on the issues of importance to us both, she should freely state her opinion so that we can come to a mutual decision. She has faithfully and absolutely "obeyed" me ever since. I am, therefore, the absolute authority in my household—technically speaking. The strategy has been a success. It works. I am still happily married. As the story of Esther unfolds, we will see whether Ahasuerus's absolute authority as king and as husband is sham or substance.

The Heroes of the Story Arrive on the Scene

At this point, the effort to sustain a view of the book of Esther as an objective, factual report of politics and policy at the Persian imperial court becomes virtually impossible. Alternatively, one can give in to the mounting force of all these clues that the story of Esther seeks not to chronicle a series of historical events but to expose the ridiculous and the preposterous—in other words, that it is farce. A six-month cocktail party, indeed! Imperial edicts to establish the proper balance of power between husband and wife, indeed! The tale continues down the path of satire:

> After these things, when the anger of King Ahasuerus had abated, he remembered Vashti and what she had done and what had been decreed against her. Then the king's servants who attended him said, "Let beautiful young virgins be sought out for the king. And let the king appoint commissioners in all the provinces of his kingdom to gather all the beautiful young virgins to the harem in the citadel of Susa under custody of Hegai,

the king's eunuch, who is in charge of the women; let their cosmetic treatments be given them. And let the girl who pleases the king be queen instead of Vashti." This pleased the king, and he did so. (2:1-4, NRSV)

Christians sometimes talk about shaping institutions in our society on the biblical model. I can well imagine that certain US presidents would favor the establishment of a "Department for Finding Beautiful Young Virgins for the President" headed by a "Secretary of Procurement," the Procurement Csar. The idea of a Miss Persia contest to choose the next queen certainly pleased King Ahasuerus. He would judge the "talent" portion of the competition himself, of course. He probably thought that it was one of the best ideas his advisors had ever had, certainly the best in the last 187 days. As is typical of the portrayal of Ahasuerus in Esther, even here, however, the king with absolute power only endorsed the ideas of his advisors. Not once does the book of Esther record that he took the initiative on anything. Half the time, he cannot even remember what he did or decreed earlier in the story and must have the officials consult the records to remind him. He seems more puppet than prince.

"Now there was a Jew in the citadel of Susa whose name was Mordecai son of Jair son of Shimei son of Kish, a Benjaminite" (2:5, NRSV). Another new character appears and introduces new dynamics. As with Ahasuerus and Vashti, the Persian sources do not mention either a Prime Minister Mordecai or a Queen Esther. In fact, their names represent problems in and of themselves as names for pious Diaspora Jews. "Mordecai" bears striking resemblance to the name of the Babylonian high god "Marduk," just as "Esther" does to the name of the Babylonian goddess "Ishtar." In any case, according to the book of Esther, Mordecai descended from the Benjaminite, Kish. It cannot be coincidental that a certain Benjaminite named Kish was the father of King Saul. The importance of this family heritage becomes clear soon.

> Mordecai had brought up Hadassah, that is Esther, his cousin, for she had neither father nor mother; the girl was fair and beautiful, and when her father and her mother died, Mordecai adopted her as his own daughter. So when the king's order and his edict were proclaimed, and when many young women were gathered in the citadel of Susa in custody of Hegai, Esther also was taken into the king's palace and put in custody of Hegai, who had charge of the women. (2:7-9 NRSV)

Esther did not reveal her ethnicity—at first an apparently insignificant detail that, like Mordecai's ancestry, will become central to events as they unfold. At any rate, Esther immediately began the procedure that she and the other candidates for the vacant queenship underwent to prepare them for their "audition" with the king. It was as exorbitant and outrageous as the extravagant royal cocktail party. "The turn came for each girl to go in to King Ahasuerus, after being twelve months under the regulations for the women, since this was the regular period of their cosmetic treatment, six months with oil of myrrh and six months with perfumes and cosmetics for women" (2:12, NRSV).

These women were meant for the king, after all. To prepare them—properly—for the king was a lengthy process. One year at the beauty parlor for one evening with the king, "unless the king delighted in her and she was summoned by name" (2:14, NRSV).

When Esther's turn came, she wisely followed the advice of Hegai, who knew the king's tastes, so she won the king's favor and was chosen to be queen to replace Vashti. To mark the occasion, of course, the king hosted a great *mishteh*, the third such cocktail extravaganza recorded in the book. By now, it should come as no surprise that he labeled it "Esther's *mishteh*" in the new queen's honor.

Subplot, Part I: Mordecai Uncovers a Coup Plan

And King Ahasuerus and Queen Esther lived happily ever after? Unfortunately, no. The book has eight more chapters, so something much more problematic than Queen Vashti's stubbornness will arise to complicate the plot. First, however, in the tradition that stretches from Shakespeare's comedies to modern sitcoms, the book of Esther introduces a subplot that will eventually weave its way back into the mainline of the story. Mordecai, who lingered around the court anonymously after Esther became queen, overheard conspirators planning to assassinate the king and dutifully reported it. After an investigation, the king had the conspirators hanged on the gallows. At first glance, this episode, recorded in only three verses, seems insignificant and unrelated to the continuation of the story. In fact, however, it sets the stage for a climactic moment much later in the tale—a minor detail necessary for the development of the plot. We must not forget it, as the king did. It turns out to be a good thing, after all, that the whole affair was "recorded in the book of the annals of the king" (2:23).

Crisis!

The account comes to the major complication; after all, without a complication, there is no reason to tell this or any other story. Esther had attained her position of prominence and, presumably, power. Mordecai had ingratiated himself to the king. What could go wrong? The problem, a man named Haman, was a descendant of Agag, the Amalekite king whom King Saul, the son of Kish the Benjaminite, long ago spared in violation of the requirements of Holy War (1 Sam 13). Thus, a blood feud extending back centuries pitted Mordecai and Haman against one another. As it happened, King Ahasuerus promoted none other than this Haman, the son of Hammedatha, the Agagite, establishing him "above all the officials who were with him" (3:1). We would call him the prime minister. Now the stage is set for the major complication to the plot: "And all the king's servants who were at the king's gate bowed down and did obeisance to Haman; for the king had so commanded concerning him. But Mordecai did not bow down or do obeisance" (3:2, NRSV).

How does one explain Mordecai's refusal to honor the newly appointed prime minister as the king ordered? Was it a violation of the Torah for a Jew to honor a (Gentile) ruler in this manner? No. The only obvious motivation for Mordecai's behavior is hatred. It was mutual. This old feud lived on. Because Saul disobediently spared Agag, the prophet Samuel informed Saul that his disobedience meant that God would give his kingdom to another. Had Saul not spared Agag, Mordecai could potentially have been the king of Israel. He certainly was not willing to do obeisance to the Agagite, Haman. Just, fair, humane, enlightened? No. Human? Absolutely.

Soon enough, some of the royal attendants tattled on Mordecai to Haman. Incidentally, Mordecai revealed himself to be a Jew to these attendants, and, in turn, they revealed this information to Haman. As one might expect, "When Haman saw that Mordecai did not bow down or do obeisance to him, Haman was infuriated" (3:5, NRSV). One might not expect, however, that Haman would think it "beneath him to lay hands on Mordecai alone. So, having been told who Mordecai's people were, Haman plotted to destroy all the Jews, the people of Mordecai, throughout the whole kingdom of Ahasuerus" (3:6, NRSV). In order to get even with Mordecai, Haman decided to encourage genocide! He did not express hatred for the Jews; apparently he had nothing against them. But he so despised Mordecai, and for such vainglorious and petty cause, that he thought it better to wipe out an entire people for a fabricated reason than to deal with Mordecai personally! Talk about overreacting!

Haman first determined a propitious date (the 14th of Adar) for his plan by casting lots. Although in Hebrew the word for "lot" is *goral*, a plural form of *pur*, the loan word (probably from Akkadian) used in Esther, actually became the name of the Jewish holiday Purim, celebrated to commemorate events recorded later in the book. Then Haman approached the king, explaining—rather duplicitously—that "a certain people" in Ahasuerus's empire followed their own laws, disregarding the king's law. Haman recommended, therefore, that the king should not tolerate their existence. He also offered what amounted to a bounty for the lives of the Jews, whom he did not identify as such to the king: 10,000 silver talents for the royal treasury if the king were to agree to the proposal. The puppet king Ahasuerus quickly assented, and, in good Persian fashion, he and Haman decided to issue throughout the empire a decree announcing that any who so desired could, on the specified date, freely and legally murder any Jew they should choose. Of course, after issuing the decree in the king's name and with his seal "to every province in its own script and every people in its own language" (3:12), the king and his prime minister "sat down to drink" (3:15). The hard work of decreeing the deaths of thousands made them thirsty.

The Heroes Stirred to Action

Meanwhile, upon the publication of the decree in Susa, the capital city, Mordecai learned of it, of course. In mourning sackcloth and ashes, he immediately went to the palace but did not enter it because, the text says, people clothed in this manner were not permitted at court. No doubt as Mordecai intended, his behavior attracted the attention of Esther's servants, who reported it to her. She sent her uncle/cousin/foster father more suitable clothing, but he refused it. Distressed, wondering what might possibly be troubling Mordecai, Esther began a conversation with him mediated by Hathach, one of the king's eunuchs. Mordecai could not have spoken with Esther face to face because she was secluded in the harem, after all. Through the messenger, Mordecai informed Esther of the decree, even sending her a copy of it, and instructed the messenger to tell Esther, who was, after all, the queen, to intervene on behalf of her people with her husband, the king—which seems to be a perfectly sensible and simple solution. But Esther replied—again through the messenger—that the problem was that, as everyone knew, it was a capital offense even for the queen to approach the king unless summoned. She added that, in fact, she had "not been called to come in to the king for thirty days" (4:11, NRSV). Reading between the lines, Mordecai seems to understand her to be saying something like, *"Why risk my life taking such a bold step? Have you forgotten about Vashti?"* Mordecai responded, somewhat harshly, that her life was already at risk, even though her ethnicity had apparently not yet been revealed: "Do not think that in the king's palace you will escape any more than all the other Jews. For if you keep silence at such a time as this, relief and deliverance will rise for the Jews from another quarter, but you and your father's family will perish. Who knows? Perhaps you have come to royal dignity for just such a time as this" (4:13-14 NRSV).

In other words, Mordecai suggested that, fortuitously, all the events leading to Esther's selection as queen may have worked out precisely so that Persia had a Jewish queen in the moment of the Jews' great crisis. Mordecai conveniently did not raise the issue that if Esther had not become queen, he would not have been spending so much time around the court and would not have come into conflict with Haman. Nor did he admit that if he had only paid respect—even grudgingly—to Haman's office, if he could bring himself to honor Haman personally, this situation would not have developed in the first place. *"The decree has been issued, Esther,"* he said, *"and if anyone is going to be able to do something to stop the mass murder of Jews, you and me included, it is you, the queen. You excelled above all those other beauties; you know what the king likes; figure something out. Do something!"*

Esther's Plan: Cocktail Parties—What Else?

She did. What method did she adopt? In the book of Esther, what else but a *mishteh*! It seems that King Ahasuerus was intoxicated all the way through the book! Drunken puppet king Ahasuerus! A couple of days later, in her royal robes, Esther stood just outside the throne room in the hallway—a clever technique to avoid committing a capital crime—where she caught the king's eye. He summoned her into his presence and asked, "What is it, Queen Esther? What is your request? It shall be given you, even to the half of my kingdom" (5:3, NRSV). Now, in a normal context, not in a farce, one would expect Queen Esther to respond to the generous offer of up to half of the kingdom (Ahasuerus must have really been smitten with her) by simply and straightforwardly stating her request: *"I want you to rescind the decree condemning the Jews, who, incidentally, are my people."* He would likely have said, *"Okay,"* and the story would have been over. The story is comic precisely because such straightforwardness never occurs. Mordecai could have nodded to Haman. Esther could have made her ethnicity publicly known. Ahasuerus could have asked Haman for more detail concerning the identity of this "certain people" whom Haman so desperately hated. Here, Esther could simply have stated her request. If any of those obvious choices had been made, however, this story would have no plot! It depends on the ridiculous. The comic has a prophetic, truth-telling dimension, and the truth is that human beings often do not do the obvious thing. People, especially inebriated puppet kings, do the ridiculous thing.

In this moment, Esther certainly did not ask for the obvious. Instead, she invited Ahasuerus *and Haman* to a *mishteh*. Perhaps we should not be surprised. The king sent for Haman and they went together to Esther's cocktail party. "While they were drinking wine" (this was a *mishteh*, not a "banquet"—there was no roast beef, no green beans, no mashed potatoes), the king repeated his question about Esther's petition and his promise to grant it, up to and including half the kingdom. Surely Esther would now state her request; it would be ridiculous not to! Instead, however, she invited the king and the prime minister to yet another *mishteh* the next day. This is the book of Esther the cocktail queen, after all. *"I invited you to this cocktail party because I wanted to use it as the opportunity to invite you to another cocktail party tomorrow."* Of course, Ahasuerus and Haman accepted Esther's invitation. Logically, Esther's actions make no sense. In the world of farce, on the other hand, as yet another in the long sequence of cocktail parties, they serve to delay the denouement, they exemplify excess, they amuse and bemuse. Above all, however, they are a plot device that sets the stage for the central episode in the book.

Plot Lines Converge at the Center

As we have seen, three plot lines run concurrently through the book: the good fortune of the beautiful Esther, Ahasuerus's new queen; the personal animosity between Haman and Mordecai; and the resultant danger facing the Jews. They intertwine in the events that take place *between* the two *mishtehs* that Esther hosted for Ahasuerus and Haman. In other words, these *mishtehs* are like parentheses around the central events, setting them up and setting them apart. The larger question of the danger facing the Jews will be resolved later. The interlude between the *mishtehs* will involve the resolution of the Haman and Mordecai plot line and will require nearly two full chapters of the book, chapters located almost precisely at its center. These events, then, are quite literally central to the story. They are pivotal.

The focus shifts now to Haman. On the surface, ironically, things could hardly be going better for Haman. Not only did he have many sons and wealth enough to purchase the extermination of an entire people, but the king had just appointed him prime minister and granted his request to exact vengeance on a hated enemy. Indeed, as the *piece de resistance*, the queen had now invited him, not once but twice, to private cocktail parties with the king. Apparently, he had been such a charming guest that Queen Esther wanted to host him again—tomorrow. It is no wonder that, inebriated and drunk with power, "Haman went out that day happy and in good spirits" (5:9, NRSV). Everything was going Haman's way, or almost everything. On his way home, he happened to pass by Mordecai who, as usual, refused to offer any gesture of respect. Haman was enraged. How dare this upstart Jew so insult the prime minister of the Persian Empire, the favorite of the new queen?

Still, Haman took no overt action. Instead, assembling his wife, Zaresh, and some of his closest friends and advisors, he consulted them with regard to the course of action he might take to exact personal revenge on Mordecai. The planned mass murder of the Jews would not satisfy his rage against Mordecai personally. As he lamented to them, all of his wealth, achievement, and status meant nothing to him *"as long as I have to see that sorry son-of-a-gun Mordecai sitting at the king's gate taunting me with disrespect every day when I leave work at the palace"* (5:11-13). Zaresh suggested that Haman simply get rid of Mordecai. *"Have a gallows fifty cubits high constructed. In the morning, get the king to have Mordecai hanged on it. Then you can go to the cocktail party unperturbed and fully enjoy the rewards of your hard work and prestige,"* she recommended (5:14). Of course, if Haman were to succeed in having Mordecai executed, there would be no reason for the planned mass murder of the Jews, but the book of Esther tends to overlook such logical considerations.

By definition, a cubit is the span from the elbow to the tip of the middle finger, or roughly fifteen to eighteen inches, a foot and a half. Fifty cubits would be approximately seventy-five feet, or seven and a half stories. Overnight? Overkill? Outrageous? Was the plan to dangle Mordecai seventy-five feet off the ground until he died or to drop him seventy-five feet? Assuming that Mordecai was of average height even by today's standards, seven-and-a-half-foot gallows would be high enough to accomplish the objective and would be much more easily, cheaply, and quickly constructed. Simply put, Zaresh's three-phased plan is ridiculous, farcical: First, build a gallows seventy-five feet high *tonight.* Second, hang Mordecai *tomorrow morning.* Third, go merrily to Esther's cocktail party *tomorrow afternoon.* Haman liked the idea, nonetheless. He ordered the construction of the gallows. Next, he would approach the king regarding the execution of Mordecai.

Meanwhile, in a typical comic turn of events, King Ahasuerus was having trouble sleeping back at the palace, so he asked to have his records read to him. Perhaps, somewhere in the back of his mind, the sense that he had left something unattended was disturbing his sleep; perhaps he could think of nothing as likely to lull him to sleep as listening to the reading of his annals; perhaps the palace staff did not include an overnight bartender to arrange a quick *mishteh*! Whatever the case, the reader came to the record of the palace intrigue that Mordecai had thwarted. The king asked what he had done to reward Mordecai for his loyalty. *"According to the records,"* the reader said, *"you did nothing."* *"Nothing? Nothing at all?"* (6:3).

At that moment, Haman arrived with the intention of initiating phase two of Zaresh's plan. *"Glad you are here, Haman,"* Ahasuerus said. *"I need some advice from my prime minister. What would be an appropriate way to honor a person whom I wish to truly honor?"* (6:6). Things kept getting better for Haman, or so he thought. *"Surely the person the king has in mind is none other than me!"* Haman suggested,

> [L]et royal robes be brought, which the king has worn, and a horse that the king has ridden, with a royal crown on its head. Let the robes and the horse be handed over to one of the king's most noble officials; let him robe the man whom the king wishes to honor, and let him conduct the man on horseback through the open square of the city, proclaiming before him: "Thus shall it be done for the man whom the king wishes to honor." (6:8-9, NRSV)

Haman stopped just short of asking for the throne—and the queen. Did Ahasuerus recognize Haman's audacity? Amazingly, Ahasuerus endorsed these measures. Of course, we remember that, in the book of Esther, the king did not *have* "yes-men"; the king *was* the "yes-man"! One can only imagine how excited Haman must have been—until the second part of the puppet king's response: *"Yes, indeed, do just that—make it so—for Mordecai!"* What a precipitous turn of the tide! Haman had come to the king to ask that his archenemy Mordecai be hanged on the specially constructed, seventy-five-foot gallows only to find himself leading the king's horse throughout the streets of the capital city with Mordecai in the saddle, wearing the king's robes and crown, while Haman proclaimed Mordecai's valor. Ahasuerus had not ordered Mordecai's execution but had instead commanded Haman to give the ancient equivalent of a ticker-tape parade in Mordecai's honor.

The unraveling of Zaresh's plan and Haman's hopes for revenge picks up pace now. Crestfallen, Haman returned home to report his failure to his wife, who ominously informed him that "If Mordecai . . . is a Jew, you will not prevail, but you will fall to him" (6:13, my translation). In effect, when it was too late, Zaresh said, *"He's a Jew? You didn't tell me he is a Jew. You should have told me. I would never have suggested that you tangle with a Jew. Oh, man. Are you in for it!"* Her statement harks back all the way to Jacob's overnight struggle with the mysterious figure at the ford of the Jabbok when Jacob's name was changed to Israel, because, as the figure said, "You have striven with God and with human beings and have prevailed" (Gen 32:28, NRSV). In fact, according to a popular etymology, the name Israel means something like "wrestled with God." For readers familiar with the Bible, Zaresh ironically (that is, whether she knew it or not) hinted that Haman had gotten into a struggle with the descendants of a man who wrestled with God and lived to tell about it. How could Haman have hoped to prevail in such a contest?

This interlude episode fulfills several functions. It has heightened the reader's suspenseful expectation concerning events to take place at the second *mishteh*. Will Esther finally get around to stating her true request? Haman's failed—doomed, according to Zaresh—efforts to exact personal vengeance on Mordecai hint at a reversal of Haman's fortunes, which to this point have been in the ascendancy. Conversely, the measures Ahasuerus took to honor Mordecai, measures that Haman inadvertently suggested and had to perform himself, hint that Mordecai had begun an ascent to prominence, wealth, and power. Literally, Haman had been given enough rope to hang himself, and, as the pace of the story picks up from this point, he reels it in, knots it, and observes that it makes a nice necktie!

Esther's Second Cocktail Party: Finally, Resolution!

After the failed plan to have Mordecai hanged, the book narrates events at Esther's second *mishteh*. At long last, Esther revealed her request to the king. She explained to him that someone in his court had been so disloyal as to trick the king into enacting a decree that would allow the annihilation of a group of his subjects who were among the most loyal and the most productive in the empire. They were a real asset to Persia. Of course, the king asked her to identify the deceiver and the people in question, but—inexplicably except as a plot device—he stormed angrily from the room before she could answer. Haman desperately fell prostrate on the couch where the queen was reclining and pled for her mercy. The king returned and interpreted Haman's act as an attack on the queen, perhaps even as sexual assault.

The immediate outcome? Well, as it happened, there was a brand new gallows located conveniently across from Haman's house that had never been used. Enraged, the king ordered that Haman be hanged on his own gallows! He was no longer a threat to Esther, Mordecai, and all the Jews, but the decree still stood. King Ahasuerus reminded Esther that Persian laws could not be rescinded—a claim that does not seem to be historically accurate but that is necessary for the development of the plot. Esther suggested that the king simply issue another decree proclaiming that, on a specific date prior to the date already established for the sanctioned mass murder of Jews, Jews could preemptively kill those who planned later to kill Jews. Naturally, just as he always agreed to requests and accepted advice, the king acceded to the queen's petition.

The Hebrew here is wonderful. It employs the only occurrence of a verb form of the word "Jew" found anywhere in the Bible. Grammatically, it is a *hithpael* stem (for those who understand these things) that is either passive or reflexive and, at the same time, causative or intensive. When the new decree was issued, the story says, hosts of Persians all across the empire "caused themselves to become Jews" the day before the Jews were to be permitted to kill their enemies, which was a couple of days before these enemies were to be permitted to kill Jews (8:17). In droves, potential Jew-haters "made Jews of themselves." Convoluted? Comic? (Just imagine all the hasty circumcisions required). Comic! Thus, the Jewish holiday of Purim was born, its observance regulated by imperial decree.

How Far Does the Farce Go?

Here, however, the problem of interpretation presented by the book of Esther reaches critical mass. Despite the many "who made Jews of themselves" throughout the Persian Empire, according to the book of Esther, Jews throughout the empire nonetheless preemptively slaughtered more than 75,000 of their enemies during two successive days of retribution. Of course, Persian history does not record any such event. More to the point, such violent vengeance constitutes a significant theological problem. Because of its apparent vengefulness, the great Reformer, Martin Luther, even considered the book of Esther unworthy of the canon.[1] As recorded in the Babylonian Talmud, the early Jewish rabbis had already recognized the difficulty presented by the book of Esther.

Rav Shmuel Bar Yehuda said, "Esther sent a message to the Sages, 'Place me in Jewish memory for all generations!' [The] Sages [responded], 'Your story would incite the nations against us.' Esther [responded], '[It's too late for that.] My story is already recorded in the chronicles of Medean and Persian kings'" (*Meg.* 7A).

Does the book of Esther endorse the idea of preemptive violence? If read as a farce, the better question may be to ask whether the umbrella of farce clearly established in the early portions of the book also extends to the accounts of the vengeful actions of Esther, Mordecai, and the Jews throughout the Persian Empire. As the Jewish Sages recorded in the Talmud recognized, only the direction of the hatred distinguishes the events that the book of Esther assigns to the original Purim from the actions Haman had planned against the Jews. In the logic of retribution, every act of revenge is always a new cause for revenge. Feuds rage for generations, long past any active memory of their origins. Farcically, Esther reverses the logic. Under the leadership of Esther and Mordecai, Persian Jews do not avenge a wrong done them. Instead, they take preemptive measures. What would have happened had a new young woman won King Ahasuerus's favor away from Esther and asked him to issue yet a third edict, decreeing that the enemies of the Jews could freely take vengeance on the Jews *the day before* the Purim edict was to take effect? In the logic of preemptive retribution, any potential offense can be the cause for a new preemptive strike: preempting the preemption. What a ridiculous notion!

In the end, it is no wonder, after all, that the book of Esther does not even mention God. The book of Esther portrays the farcical absurdity of cocktail party empires, cocktail party queens, cocktail party decrees, and cocktail party vengeance. God does not endorse such displays of pomposity and power. God is not the bartender in the book of Esther. The book of Esther does not ratify violence—either Persian or Jewish. It does not endorse revenge. It ridicules imperial decrees, whether drafted by Haman or Mordecai. It ridicules puppet kings and power-drunk Persian ministers of state. It exposes the ineffectiveness of male power confronted by a beautiful, clever, determined wife.

Farce and Survival—Theology and Empire

Why would an oppressed minority, living under foreign occupation or in a Diaspora abroad, delight in such a depiction of Persian debauchery and foolhardiness and of Jewish vengeance? What function might such satire serve? Does it give anyone hope? Why does it belong in the Bible? The question answers itself. Remembering that, beginning in 587/6 BCE and continuing until 1947, the Jews in Palestine/Israel were subject to the domination of one empire after another—first the Assyrian, then the Babylonian, then the Persian, then the Greek, and then the Roman—and that they were subject to decrees such as Antiochus IV Epiphanes' ridiculous order banning the observance of the Sabbath, we must consider the fact that the Jewish people had to find ways to survive as a perpetual minority. Indeed, stretching back to the beginnings of Israel, they had been a single family wandering among the Canaanites, then a people in bondage to perhaps the first great empire, Egypt. Prior to the modern era, they knew political autonomy only for the brief period of the few centuries of the monarchy—and even then, Israel was plagued by the territorial and cultural incursions of the Philistines, Moabites, Ammonites, Edomites, Amalekites, etc. The Israel that produced the book of Esther knew well what it was to be enslaved, oppressed, and disenfranchised. In fact, if Esther ostensibly makes fun of the Persian Empire and if, as many scholars think, it was written during the later Hellenistic or even the Maccabean period, then "Persia" is a cipher or code for empire.

The book of Esther asks and answers the question of how to manage life under such circumstances. You recognize how shallow the power that empire exerts actually is. You recognize the ridiculous nature of all that legal structure, that wealth, that pomp, and that presumption. How meaningless and foolish it is to think that empire can dictate the nature of the relationship between husband and wife by decree! Imperial decrees certainly cannot invalidate God's plan for God's people—as even Zaresh recognized. With this awareness, you use the very pomposity of empire against itself. If nothing else, you use it as the source for your own strength. One can quickly render inert the power of an enemy by recognizing its flaws and—perhaps privately and perhaps openly—ridiculing it. One can remember that the government cannot compel one to abandon one's identity. The powerful can harm me physically, but they cannot reach into my mind or my heart. The powerful can force me to commit an external act, but they cannot force me to think and believe as they wish me to think and believe. Indeed, no one can truly know what is in my heart and mind except God. Issue your silly decrees; you only reveal your impotence over my heart and mind, over my identity.

In fact, Jewish practice confirms this reading of Esther as a farce ridiculing imperial power. Since the beginning, Jewish tradition has observed Purim as a time of farce. Oddly, unlike Passover, which Christians link to Easter, and Pentecost, which Christians observe as the birthday of the church, the church has completely overlooked Purim. To this day, Purim celebration resembles a combination of April Fool's Day, Thanksgiving, May Day, and harvest festival. During the reading of the book of Esther in the synagogue, children use noisemakers and adults stamp their feet every time Haman's name is read aloud. It is a time for masquerading, feasting, gifts, and partying. The rabbis used to say that on Purim one should drink (*mishteh!*) until one can no longer distinguish between "Cursed be Haman!" and "Blessed be Mordecai!" Party hardy! Mardi Gras! Many churches would benefit from an injection of the Purim party spirit. Many Christians would benefit, too, from the ability to view the world with the eyes of farce. Much that seems serious is only ostentation.

One element of the genius of the Baptist view of the church resonates with Esther's farcical view of empire. While the many varieties of Baptists differ on many things—else there would not be varieties of Baptists—the core Baptist understanding that the church consists of baptized believers defines them all. This core belief implies that the church and the "world" are not identical and, short of the consummation of God's kingdom, cannot be so. The church, Baptists argue, exists *within* the world, but the world has no real power over the church. Indeed, the exercise of coercive power, the issuance of decrees to govern matters of faith and conscience, is an imperial practice, inconsistent with the methods of sacrificial love and service. Historically, Baptists have expressed this insight in the call for the separation of church and state. Seen through the lens of the book of Esther, this separation must mean more than the important idea that the state should refrain from mixing into the affairs of religion; it must also mean that the community of faith should bear witness to its experience of God and its understanding of reality but must not use the tools of worldly power to do so. How quickly the liberated slave can become another pharaoh!

For thirty years or so, Baptists in the American South have struggled with the realization that the cultural hegemony they once exercised has fractured. The struggle to come to peace with that reality has involved moaning and bemoaning, efforts to reassert cultural dominance through legislation, and, unfortunately, a significant proportion of internecine warfare. Ironically, the period of the cultural dominance of Baptists and other Free Church and evangelical Christians in the South coincided with the period of racial injustice that so mars American history and, especially, that so scars the church even today. Roger Williams, Obadiah Holmes, John Leland . . . what would they say about their descendants in the faith? Baptists have always laughed at power structures. Real power is in relationship with God and in living a life that emulates God's love—God's power. All else is but farce!

Note

1. "For you poke more than a little sarcastic fun at this when you compare Proverbs and The Song of Solomon (which with a sneering innuendo you call the "Love Song") with the two books of Esdras, Judith, the story of Susanna and the Dragon, and Esther (which despite their [the Jews'] inclusion of it in the canon deserves more than all the rest in my judgment to be regarded as noncanonical)" (Martin Luther, *The Bondage of the Will*, trans. J. I. Packer and O. R. Johnston, Grand Rapids MI: Revell, 1957; repr. 1999) 143 (=*LW* 33:110).

Chapter 5

Jesus: The Incarnate Wit of God

"Back of every mistaken venture and defeat is the laughter of wisdom, if you listen." (Carl Sandburg)

Those old enough to recall the 1984 and 1988 presidential campaigns probably do not remember the electoral college results, the major policy positions of the leading candidates, or even the most successful campaign ads, but they will probably have no difficulty recalling two humorous moments in the televised debates, one in each campaign. The first happened in the debate between presidential candidates Ronald Reagan and Walter Mondale in the 1984 campaign. The second occurred in a debate between vice-presidential candidates Lloyd Bentsen and Dan Quayle in the 1988 election. Coincidentally, both moments related to the merits of life experience and wisdom as a function of age versus the value of energy and vigor as a function of youth. In 1984, Ronald Reagan, at the time already the oldest president in history, attempted to defuse concerns about his relatively advanced age with the whimsical statement, "I want you to know that also I will not make age an issue of this campaign. I am not going to exploit, for political purposes, my opponent's youth and inexperience." Four years later, Senator Quayle responded to a question as to whether his youth diminished his stature as a candidate for the office first in succession for the presidency by comparing himself to President Kennedy. Off the cuff, Senator Bentsen retorted, "I knew Jack Kennedy. Jack Kennedy was a friend of mine. Senator, you're no Jack Kennedy."

Battles of Wit

Both comments typify the riposte, the retort, the snappy comeback common in contexts ranging from the playground to the presidential debate stage. Like all humor, such comments exploit, or in the examples cited, *assert* a fundamental incongruity (in both examples, the incongruous desire to find in one person both youthful vigor and mature wisdom). These comeback

lines serve a number of functions in social interaction. They invite the target
to join in a verbal fencing match. The party unable to respond quickly or
unable to respond with equal wit loses the contest. Minimally, the winning
riposte demonstrates the superior wit of the speaker and may be considered
a demonstration of the accuracy of the implicit assertion. Sometimes the
loser even admits "defeat" ("You got me on that one!").

The purposes of such battles of wit can range from the social cohesion
that results from playful banter among friends to more aggressive attempts
to expose a weakness in an opponent's argument or even to diminish the
opponent before an audience. Often, whether in the context of a gathering
of friends or in more formal debate settings, an audience functions as arbiter
and judge of the contest. These verbal exchanges are for show. In terms of
the presidential debates cited as examples, in fact, the witticisms clearly
targeted the voting public. They were, in effect, attacks on an opponent's
qualifications for office clothed in humor so as both to sharpen the incongruity and to shield the attacker from the appearance of meanness and
aggression.

Significantly, in fact, rejoinders such as Bentsen's and Reagan's play no
roles in a true conversation between opposing parties. Both made their comments in the context of a *debate* not a *discussion*. Such remarks do not function to persuade a dialogue partner, who is presumably committed to a
position, but to influence an audience. Indeed, they function in a rhetorical
strategy that objectifies the apparent conversation partner. In actuality, the
conversation takes place between the wit and the audience. The witticism
invites the audience to recognize the speaker as the superior and to agree
that the incongruity posited in the riposte accurately describes reality.

Jesus' Battles of Wit with His Opponents

The dialogues between Jesus and his opponents—the scribes, Pharisees,
Sadducees, and Herodians—recorded in the Gospels exhibit all these characteristics of the challenge of wits. Usually, Jesus' opponents initiated the
exchange with a question designed to entrap Jesus and expose him as a
heterodox teacher or lax practitioner of the law as he stood before an audience of people assembled to hear him teach and see him perform wonders.
Rather than fall haplessly victim, however, in every case recorded in the
Gospels Jesus demonstrated his superiority in a rejoinder that minimally
silenced his opposition and, more pointedly, revealed them to be incompe-
tent theologians and debaters. These exchanges amazed and delighted the
public audience, but they also angered the humiliated religious leadership

and constituted a major factor, according to Mark (3:6) and Matthew (12:9),[1] that motivated Jesus' enemies to seek his execution. They wanted to silence this voice that consistently undermined their status and authority in the eyes of the public.

A Preliminary Word of Caution

Before turning to specific examples from Mark, the oldest Gospel and the model for the other Synoptics,[2] a word of caution regarding interpreting these passages in ways that tend toward anti-Semitism is in order. It is important to remember that, although Jesus exposed his opponents to ridicule and even occasionally attacked them directly, calling them "a brood of vipers," for example (Matt 3:7; 12:34; 23:33; Luke 3:7), Jesus did not thereby mount a blanket attack on Jews as an ethnicity or Judaism as a religion. To be sure, these scribes, Pharisees, Sadducees, and Herodians were Jews, but so were Jesus, Jesus' disciples, the public Jesus addressed indirectly in these disputes with the religious leadership, and many members of the early church that constituted Mark's audience. In fact, the Judaism of Jesus' day—like the Judaism of today, or like any faith tradition for that matter—was far from uniform. The Pharisees disagreed with the Sadducees, and both disagreed with the Zealots. The average Palestinian laborer did not have the luxury of the time or money needed to undertake the in-depth study of Scripture, to engage in scholarly discussion, or to observe the meticulous practice encouraged by the Pharisees, for example. Furthermore, these Pharisees, Jesus' chief opponents on matters of biblical interpretation according to the Gospels, disagreed among themselves on a number of important issues. Jesus did not condemn Sadduceeism or Pharisaism per se; Jesus came to call people into the kingdom of God, not to reject one theological school of thought or endorse another. Indeed, individual Pharisees became disciples (Nicodemus, James the brother of Jesus, Paul), presumably without ceasing to be Pharisees and certainly without ceasing to be Jews. These debates (scholars prefer "disputations" as a more precise technical term) involved one Jewish rabbi disagreeing with other Jewish rabbis concerning the proper interpretation of Scripture, the proper form of Judaism, and the proper practice of biblical faith. Jesus' accusation against the religious leadership of his day must not be inflated into attacks against an entire ethnic group or religion.

Early Suspicions: The Seed for Later Opposition

According to Mark's account, religious leaders were suspicious of Jesus almost from the outset of his ministry, and their suspicions quickly blossomed into outright opposition and animosity. Mark reports that, after his baptism and temptation, Jesus began preaching the good news in Galilee (1:14-15), called his first disciples (1:16-19), and exorcised an unclean spirit in Capernaum, an act that brought Jesus fame (1:21-28) and attracted crowds (1:29-34), before he set out on a preaching tour of the region (1:35-39). Mark then relates a series of incidents that make it clear that Jesus' fame grew rapidly—and also attracted the attention of the religious leadership. Indeed, the news of the healing of a leper drew such large crowds that Jesus was forced to work in the open countryside (1:40-45). After returning to Capernaum, Jesus was teaching in an overcrowded home when four entrepreneurial men lowered their paralytic friend through the roof into the middle of the room. In response to their faith, Jesus forgave the man's sin, and the first indication of tensions between Jesus and the religious establishment surfaced.

"Certain of the scribes" seated among those listening to Jesus teach speculated privately whether Jesus' bold pronouncement of forgiveness did not amount to blasphemy since only God can forgive sin (2:6-7). In their view, Jesus was making grand proclamations, but they wondered whether he was capable of anything more than just talk. Anyone can claim to forgive sins: there is no observable evidence. Somehow, Mark says, Jesus knew what they were thinking and chose to challenge their objections directly. He asked, "Which is easier, to say to the paralytic, 'Your sins are forgiven,' or to say 'Take up your bed and walk'?" Notably, Jesus' detractors did not answer the question, probably because there is no answer to it. It borders on the ridiculous. To heal a sinner's heart or to heal a paralytic's legs are both well beyond normal human capacities. Jesus prefaced what he was about to do with the explanation, "So that you may know that the Son of Man has authority on earth to forgive sins . . . ." In other words, Jesus accepted the challenge. *"Okay. I'll give you observable evidence of my authority. Watch this!"* Turning to the paralytic, Jesus instructed him, "Take up your bed and go home." When the man did so, everyone assembled was, of course, amazed. Clearly, Jesus was much more than a big talker.

Jesus' words and deeds did not, however, persuade the scribes; they seem rather to have accomplished the contrary. When Jesus next called a tax collector, Levi, as the fifth disciple, "the scribes of the Pharisees" dared for the first time to voice openly their accusatory question concerning why Jesus consorted with such disreputable and despicable sinners, although they spoke to Jesus' disciples instead of going directly to him (2:16). Jesus overheard the question and explained his actions by cleverly comparing himself to the physician who heals the sick, not the well (2:17). The Pharisees, and even John's disciples, apparently had reservations not only about the company Jesus kept but also about his behavior, noting that Jesus and his disciples, who "ate with sinners" (cf. Matt 11:19, where Jesus quotes the accusation against him that he partied too much, that he was "a glutton and a drunkard") and did not fast as any pious teacher should, in their view. In short, they implied that this rabbi who partied with sinners was guilty of impiety. Jesus responded with another pithy saying suggesting that, in fact, it was party time; the time for fasting (and mourning) would come soon enough (2:19-20). Thus, these two early encounters between Jesus and a growing opposition contain the seeds for the open conflict that will mature in Jesus' crucifixion.

Public Debates Round One: The Sabbath

The tension between Jesus and the establishment emerges into the open in the next episode of Mark's account only two chapters into the Gospel. This passage, the first report of a full-blown debate/disputation, not only suggests by its placement that opposition to Jesus arose early in his public ministry but also demonstrates clearly that the fundamental issue dividing Jesus and his chief opponents, (some of) the Pharisees, involved disagreement concerning the proper approach to interpreting the Bible. In other words, they did not disagree about the canonical authority of the Law (and the Prophets) but about how to understand it. Furthermore, of course, it offers a parade example of our primary interest, Jesus' retort style of argumentation and, perhaps surprisingly, of his willingness to *provoke* his enemies—to make fun of them!

Plucking Grain (Mark 2:23-28)

While the point of controversy in this episode is clear, Jesus' reasoning by way of an example phrased as a rhetorical question addressed to his opponents requires explication. Traveling on the Sabbath by foot through a grain field, Jesus' disciples plucked (and presumably ate) a few heads of grain. The Pharisees apparently traveling with them asked pointedly why Jesus' disciples were violating the commandment against working, in this case by harvesting, on the Sabbath. The question implies that either their teacher had indulged them in their wrongdoing, had failed to teach them adequately, or had, in fact, taught them incorrectly. Significantly, the Pharisees did not object to the disciples' actions on the grounds that they constituted theft, because the Mosaic law makes provision for travelers to sustain themselves in such a manner (Deut 23:25). From the Pharisees' perspective, the case was open and closed. Jesus may have countered their earlier doubts about his authority to forgive sins by healing the paralytic, and he may have muted their complaints about the company he kept and his celebration of life by citing witty proverbs, but now Jesus' disciples had blatantly violated an explicit prohibition in the Decalogue, and Jesus had either permitted it, condoned it, or encouraged it. Jesus' opponents thought that they had caught him red-handed! Jesus not only consorted with sinners; his *disciples* were sinners, and Jesus may have been a false teacher, a sinner, himself!

Their attitude typifies an approach to Scripture and ethics still around today that views the rules as sacrosanct and absolute. The rules must be strictly observed under all circumstances. For these Pharisees (but not necessarily for all Pharisees), rules were more important than the needs of people. Indeed, for these Pharisees, the rules were more potent than the God who made them. Jesus' scriptural example and his explicit statement that the Sabbath was made for humankind, not vice versa, indicates that, in contrast, he viewed the commandments not as an end unto themselves but as a means for shaping a rich and meaningful life in fellowship with God and with one another. In other words, Jesus argued that God gave the commandments to benefit human beings, not to burden them with otherwise meaningless obligations.

These Pharisees remind me of my children's attitude toward the rule in our household against running down the hallway. The children thought that their mother and I imposed this rule and many others just to deprive them of fun or to give us an opportunity to test their obedience. They thought the rules were arbitrary. Of course, we intended the rules to protect and nurture, to substitute for the wisdom the children would gain with maturity. Specifically, we intended the rule against running down the hallway to prevent damage to the house and its furnishings and, more importantly, injuries to members of the household. When one of the children slammed into a sibling rounding the corner at the far end of the hallway, necessitating stitches, the very possibility the rule hoped to forestall, they caught on. Similarly, Jesus argued, God did not make rules just to test human obedience. Instead, the rules are for the benefit of humanity. God revealed the principles for living an authentic human life. Since the essential principle underlying the Sabbath commandment involves rest that sustains life, Jesus argued that to observe the Sabbath prohibition against work even if it means going hungry would be nonsensical and contrary to the purpose of the Sabbath, namely to preserve and enrich life.

The way Jesus made the point to his opponents is striking. Rather than answer the question, Jesus laid his own trap for them. Jesus' tactic here and in the other disputes involves questions crafted such that his opponents dare not answer them either yes or no. They are comparable to questions such as the gag one sometimes hears, "So, have you stopped beating your wife?" A yes answer implies that you were formerly guilty of habitual spousal abuse; a no response suggests that you are still engaged in the behavior. In this case, moreover, Jesus did not even permit his opponents an opportunity to answer, dismissively implying that, although they claimed to be authorities on Scripture, they lacked sufficient familiarity with it ("Have you not read . . . ?"). The question itself recalls an episode in David's life (1 Sam 22) when, as a fugitive from Saul, he required sustenance. The priests at Nob provided it to him in the form of the bread kept in the sanctuary as a symbol of God's presence in accordance with the law of Moses (Exod 25:30; 35:13; 39:36; Num 4:7), bread too sacred for laypersons such as David to consume. The priests at Nob, experts in the law charged with administering the sanctuary, valued David's life over ritual regulations! Did Jesus' pharisaical opponents share the values of the venerable priests at Nob? Obviously, the Pharisees were not prepared to concede Jesus' point, and they could not object that David had, with the collusion of the priests at Nob, in fact violated a commandment. The Pharisees and, more important, the people held David in too high regard. They certainly could not contend that the priests at Nob should have permitted David to starve. Incidentally, Jesus may have built an additional trap into his question involving the Pharisees' familiarity with Scripture. As Mark tells the story, Jesus named Abiathar as the high priest at Nob when, according to 1 Samuel 21:1, it was actually Ahimelech, Abiathar's father. Either Mark supplied the name from memory (neither Matthew nor Luke mentions the high priest by name), Jesus made a mistake (which is highly unlikely), or Jesus was testing the Pharisee's Bible knowledge.

The Pharisees' silence spoke volumes. They did not catch the error, and they certainly were not interested in open dialogue about the substance of the situation. They only wanted to trap Jesus. They not only missed the opportunity to point out a minor problem with a detail in Jesus' argument but also had no answer for Jesus' logic. In fact, as it turned out, Jesus had them cornered. *"Pharisees, I know the Bible, and I know that the priests at Nob chose to save David's life rather than insist on keeping a rule. They valued human life more than rules. They recognized that the point of the rules is to value life! You are not like the priests at Nob."*

Gotcha!

Healing (Mark 3:1-6)

Jesus confronted his opponents even more aggressively in the episode Mark records next. Again, the conflict between the Sabbath prohibition against work—in this case healing a man with a paralyzed hand—and the fundamental Sabbath value of restoring and nurturing life became the fulcrum. The Pharisees and Herodians considered the presence of a paralytic in the synagogue on the Sabbath fortuitous bait for entrapping Jesus. If true to his pattern of behavior so far in his ministry, Jesus might well heal the man if asked to do so. A new trap was set—but for whom? Jesus fully recognized the implications of the situation and went on the offensive without waiting for his opponents to reveal their intentions. Jesus did not even wait for the paralytic to ask for help. Instead, Jesus instructed him to stand up "in the midst" of the synagogue worshipers—to take center stage, as it were—and then he posed another "gotcha!" question to his enemies: If the Sabbath is God's good and restorative gift, a testament to God's liberating act of freeing Israel from Egyptian bondage (cf. Deut 5:14-15), should one do good on the Sabbath—should one emulate the God who frees from bondage by freeing a paralytic from his paralysis—or should one perpetuate harm by doing nothing? Would the prohibition against work require one to refuse to bandage a child in danger of bleeding to death on the Sabbath?

As in the previous example, Jesus left his enemies with no good option. They could either acquiesce, admitting that Jesus had correctly interpreted the law—which they were determined not to do—or they could take the ridiculous stance that the Sabbath can be an excuse for permitting harm, if "only" by refusing to act when action would otherwise be in order. *"Do you suggest that, in order to observe the Sabbath rigorously, we should close all the hospitals one day a week? Do you think that heart attacks will take the day off, too? Should we give firefighters a holiday? Surely you know that fire won't observe the Sabbath, don't you?"* Jesus had painted them into a corner. They looked ridiculous. It is little wonder, then, that "they kept silent," that their dishonest silence angered Jesus, and that Jesus promptly healed the paralytic man.

"I want you to know that I will not allow your inability or unwillingness to answer a simple question to hinder me from doing the right thing. I will make your obstinacy an issue in this campaign." The silence of Jesus' opponents demonstrated that they had no interest in true dialogue, although they had no effective counter-argument; they had decided. Jesus had to die. The only question they were willing to discuss among themselves, therefore, was how to accomplish it (3:6). Remarkably, then, according to Mark, almost at the beginning of Jesus' ministry, the religious (and political, if "Herodians" refers to adherents of the ruling family) leadership—humiliated and angered by Jesus who repeatedly and publicly exposed them to ridicule, exposing the ridiculous incongruity of their position and their inability and unwillingness to engage him in honest discussion—had decided that Jesus must be eliminated. It is equally remarkable that Jesus "took it to them" so aggressively and that the contentious issues involved the principles of biblical interpretation.

Public Debates Round Two: Jesus' Authority Challenged

Mark relates no other such exchange between Jesus and his opponents until his account of Passion Week, after Jesus' triumphal entry into Jerusalem and immediately following Jesus' cleansing of the temple—an act that no doubt represented Jesus' accusation against the validity and authority of the religious establishment. In any case, when Mark returns to the theme of opposition to Jesus and his teaching in the account of Jesus' last week, he incorporates a concentrated series of disputations in 11:27–12:40, interrupted only by a parable in which Jesus attacks the religious leadership directly (12:1-12) and, oddly, the unique conversation between Jesus and a scribe concerning the greatest commandment, a discussion that stands out for its lack of animosity. Jesus even approved of the scribe who, Jesus said, was "not far from the kingdom of God" (12:34). We can be thankful to Mark for including this reminder that Jesus was not hostile toward Pharisaism, per se, or toward scribes as a group, and certainly not toward Jews as a people. Jesus' ministry announced the kingdom of God and called for love of God and of one's neighbor. Scribes and Pharisees could, and did, respond to that call, too. Nonetheless, the section ends not with a debate or a parable but with Jesus' straightforward denunciation of the scribes (12:38-40). Apparently, those who responded positively to Jesus' preaching were few indeed.

Jesus' Authority to Cleanse the Temple (Mark 11:27-33)

The first in this final series of disputations that hardened the determination of the religious leadership to rid themselves of the irritant Jesus represents perhaps the most complete example of the genre. Unlike other examples that only hint at the motivation and thought processes of the participants, this unit outlines them overtly and explicitly. Sometime after Jesus cleansed the temple, which was a clear attack on the establishment and a blatant provocation ("and the chief priests and scribes heard and were seeking how to kill him," 11:18), when Jesus returned to the temple, the chief priests and scribes confronted him, demanding to know "by what authority" he had "done this," that is, had cleansed the temple. Employing the technique of the unanswerable "gotcha" counter-question by now familiar to readers of Mark, Jesus promised to respond if they would first answer his question concerning the source of the authority of John the Baptist. *Riddle me this, Pharisees: Was John's authority heavenly or earthly, divine or human? Was John a prophet or a charlatan?* Jesus' demand, "Answer me!" (11:30), manifested his impatience with his opponents and his aggressive, confrontational attitude toward them.

The deliberation concerning how to respond to Jesus reveals once again that Jesus' enemies were not interested in seeking common ground or a deeper understanding of the truth, but only in embarrassing Jesus. The discussion reveals them to be insincere, willing—even eager—to cower to public opinion, hypocritical, and cowardly. If, on the one hand, they reasoned, they were to acknowledge John's divine commission, they would expose themselves to questions about their own failure to respond to John's call to repentance. Alternatively, since the people regarded John to be a true prophet, if they were to label him a charlatan it would only alienate the populace and cast doubt on their ability to discern God's will and work in the world, undermining their own authority as teachers and leaders. For the first and only time recorded in Mark, however, Jesus' opponents dared an answer, of sorts, to one of Jesus' "gotcha!" questions: "We do not know."

The sole glaring omission of a significant detail in this account involves the reaction of the crowds that must have gathered to hear this exchange. They were Jesus' true audience (just as readers are Mark's), after all. We can only imagine that a crowd of worshipers who heard their chief priests and theologians admit publicly that they had been unable to reach a conclusion concerning the nature of John's ministry must have been dismayed (just as Mark's readers are). How embarrassing! How this admission must have undermined the reputation of these "leaders"! The emperor wore no clothes!

Jesus certainly did not miss the opportunity to drive the point home. *"If you, of all people, do not know, I'm surely not going to tell you!"* (11:33, par-aphrased). *"It's for me to know and you to find out!"* Immediately (12:1-11), according to Mark, Jesus told the parable of the wicked tenants (the religious leadership) who withheld the fruits of the vineyard (Israel) from the landowner (God) and abused the landowner's messengers (the prophets, like John), indeed, including even his son (the Son, Jesus). Jesus' opponents held themselves out to be authorities on God's word, will, and way, but they were more concerned with public opinion than with identifying with John the Baptist and his God-ordained mission. They were not exercising their responsibility to care for God's people. They were despising God's messen-gers, both John the Baptist *and Jesus.* Mark reports that the chief priests and scribes understood the point of Jesus' parable clearly and would have arrested him on the spot if they had not been afraid of the crowd's reaction (12:12).

Roman Coins and God's Image (Mark 12:13-17)

Perhaps, Jesus' opponents thought, they could turn the tables on Jesus, using his own debate techniques to expose him to public embarrassment and ridicule for a change. A group of theologians (Pharisees) and politicians (Herodians) attempted to spring just such a trap (12:13), baited with flattery and the volatile subject of taxes paid to the hated Roman occupiers of Israel. "Teacher," they asked disingenuously, "we know that you are truthful/honest and do not care what people think or take into account a person's status/rep-utation, but (simply) teach God's way truthfully" (12:14a, my translation). Their description of Jesus as an honest man, not swayed by public opinion, contrasts ironically with their own behavior in the previous encounter. They condemned themselves out of their own mouths! After this model of flattery, we readers of the book of Mark know the mind-set of Jesus' opposition well enough to expect a humdinger of a trick question, and we will not be dis-appointed. "Is it permissible to pay Caesar's taxes or not? Shall we pay or not?" (12:14b, my translation). They had finally learned something from Jesus, it seems—unfortunately not about the kingdom of God, but only about how to set a trap in a battle of wits! Jesus could have answered in one of two ways, both dangerous. If Jesus were to have answered affirmatively that one should legitimately pay Roman taxes, then his reputation with the people would have been tarnished. They would have viewed him not as a champion of the poor but as a Roman sympathizer or, worse, a collaborator. On the other hand, if he were to have declared the Roman tax system ille-gitimate, the Roman authorities would have seen him as a nationalist, a zealot, a rebel, and would probably have arrested him immediately. *Touché!* Finally, a point for the Pharisees.

Or perhaps not. Could Jesus escape this trap? He was, after all, an expert counter-puncher. First, Jesus dismissed this apparent victory as yet another example of the obstinacy and incompetence of his enemies (12:15): "Why do you (keep) testing me (when you have been so unsuccessful in all your past efforts)?" That is, *"You just don't know when to quit, do you?"* Then, in a new twist, Jesus taught an object lesson both in how to parry a thrust in debate and in how to reason theologically. When he asked in a simple, non-threatening fashion to see a Roman coin, his opponents gave him one. Jesus had sprung the trap. Already, he had won the contest, although his opponents did not seem to realize it. They had asked him whether it is appropriate for a Jew to participate in the Roman economic system—implying, of course, that it is not and daring Jesus to contradict them publicly. When asked for a Roman coin, the currency of the Roman realm, however, they needed only to reach into their own coin purses to produce one. Politics, economics, and theology aside, in practice they were already active participants in the Roman economy. Hypocrites!

Second, Jesus saw them and raised them in this game of theological high card! His next question carries with it rich allusions and connotations: "Whose image and inscription is this?" Roman coins typically bore the emperor's image, of course, and some variation of the declaration/title "Caesar (is) lord!" In fact, Julius Caesar took for himself the name *Divus Julius,* thereby laying claim to status as a living deity. After his assassination, the Roman Senate succumbed to pressure, officially acknowledged his claim to be *divus,* and authorized his adopted son Octavian to stage a formal celebration of Julius's *apotheosis,* his elevation to divinity. The Senate granted the title and status of deity to later emperors almost as a matter of course. In essence, then, Jesus exposed the fact that his opponents—Israel's religious and political leaders—carried on their persons miniature idol images of the Roman emperor who claimed to be a god! Yet they dared to ask him a tax question!

Finally, Jesus did not stop with this public exposure of his opponents' hypocrisy (*"Go ahead! Give Caesar back the little idol image of him that you carry around in your pocket!"*) but went on quite subtly to teach a profound theological truth. Although he did not make an explicit assertion, Jesus' question about the image on the Roman coin, which employs the Greek term used in the ancient Greek translation of the Old Testament to refer to the creation of humankind in God's image and from which we get the English word "icon," calls to mind the comparison between Roman coins bearing the emperor's image and human beings bearing God's image. If Roman coins constitute the currency of the Roman realm, and therefore the Roman ruler has a legitimate claim to them, then human beings constitute the "currency" of the kingdom of God! Essentially, Jesus said, *"It's okay to give Caesar his money. Just be sure to give God your whole selves!"*

Resurrection (Mark 12:18-27)

So far, according to Mark, Jesus' primary opponents have been "the scribes and Pharisees," joined occasionally by the Herodians. Now, however, Mark indicates that opposition to Jesus extended beyond these lay and political groups to include the priests, the Sadducees. Undoubtedly, they saw Jesus' cleansing of the temple as an incursion into their territory, a challenge to their authority. Accordingly, they joined the fray. Unlike the Pharisees, who belonged to a movement or a religious party, the Sadducees constituted a class, a priestly aristocracy. They took their name, apparently, from their purported ancestor, Zadok, one of David's priests. The disputes between Jesus and the Pharisees had focused on the interpretation of the Scriptures, primarily the Law. Significantly, Jesus sometimes appealed to biblical books outside the Law, as in his reference to David and the bread of the presence. In addition to priestly status, the Sadducees differed from the Pharisees (and Jesus) not just on the interpretation of Scripture but also on the definition of it. The Sadducees considered *only* the Law, the books of Moses, canonically authoritative; that is, for them the Bible consisted only of Genesis through Deuteronomy. Furthermore, since the Law makes no obvious reference to resurrection or an afterlife, the Sadducees did not believe in the resurrection of the dead, a belief that Jesus shared with the Pharisees. Not surprisingly, then, the dispute between Jesus and the Sadducees that Mark records next hinges on precisely these two issues: the doctrine of resurrection and the exclusive authority of the books of Moses. The issues may have differed, but the Sadducees, like the Pharisees, tried to trap Jesus with a trick question—and found themselves caught in their own device.

The Sadducees approached Jesus with a cleverly constructed hypothetical situation based on the Deuteronomic law governing levirate marriage (Deut 25:5-10) and designed to expose the absurdity of the idea of resurrection. Levirate marriage provided a single solution to several problems in ancient Israelite society. Since, technically, women could not own property, and in the absence of any social security system, a childless widow faced destitution. Furthermore, a man who died childless left no heritage—either in terms of the survival of his name and lineage or in the very real terms of property. In the event a man should die leaving behind a widow but no heir, the Mosaic law calls for his brother to marry the widowed sister-in-law. In a legal fiction, the first child born of this second union was considered the child of the decedent. Voila! The dead man has a child to perpetuate his lineage and memory, an heir to his property, and a child to provide for his widow, the child's mother, in her old age. The Sadducees concocted an unlikely, even outrageous, "One Bride for Seven Brothers" levirate scenario in which, in succession, each of seven brothers marries the same woman only to die childless. Their question—"whose wife would she be in the resurrection?"—envisions the absurd possibility of seven brothers sharing one wife in heaven.

The Sadducees must have been proud of their word experiment. Readers of the book of Mark, however, as no doubt some of Jesus' regular followers would have, expect Jesus to invert the trap cleverly and decisively. In fact, he did so with a parry and a counterthrust. First, he dismissed the scenario out of hand, explaining simply that heavenly existence will not include marriage at all. He may have suggested that, ironically, the Sadducees' hypothetical situation, in fact, leads to this conclusion, not to the invalidation of the doctrine of resurrection, which was their true intent. Instead, Jesus said, people will be "like the angels." This statement is merely an assertion, however, with no obvious foundation in experience or Scripture, and would have had little capacity for refuting the Sadducees' position. Thus, Jesus pivoted and attacked the Sadducees' reasoning at its foundation: the Law, the books of Moses! At the burning bush, God identified himself to Moses with the statement, "I *am* the God of Abraham, the God of Isaac, and the God of Jacob"—*am* not *was!* The relationship between God and the three patriarchs was still in existence in the moment when God spoke to Moses. Therefore, somehow (Jesus does not elaborate), the patriarchs were still involved in relationship with God; they were still alive! God is the God of the living! Deftly, Jesus interpreted Scripture that the Sadducees agreed was authoritative to demonstrate that the doctrine of resurrection, which they rejected as unfounded in the Torah, in fact derives from God's essential self-description located at the center of the Torah. The Sadducees did not know their own Bible! Verb tense (was, am, will be) makes a great deal of difference in theology. Silly Sadducees! Jesus pronounced the outcome of the debate. The Sadducees had "erred greatly" (12:27).

Jesus the Aggressor (Mark 12:35-37)

Mark concludes this second series of disputations between Jesus and his enemies dramatically, even explosively, with the only account of Jesus aggressively initiating conflict and ultimately issuing an explicit, harsh condemnation. While teaching in the temple, Jesus posed a question, not addressed *to* the scribes but, in a rhetorical flourish likely intended to involve the audience and to exclude the scribes, *about* the scribes. *"How is it,"* he asked, *"that these scribes teach that the Messiah, the Christ, will be a descendant of David when, in Psalm 110:1, David related God's statement to someone, presumably the Messiah, whom David calls 'my lord'? What great-great-grandfather addresses his great-great-grandson as 'my lord'?"* Translation issues partially obscure the force of Jesus' question. The Greek of Mark attributes the statement Jesus cites to "the Lord," while the Hebrew of Psalm 110:1 has the divine proper name *YHWH*. The Greek of Mark uses the same word, "lord," a second time to refer to David's descendant; the Hebrew of Psalm 110:1 has the honorific title *adoni*, "my lord," here in an almost feudal sense but with no divine connotations.

In any case, Jesus did not answer his own question or explicate the psalm text further. He obviously implied that, in the case of the Messiah, the descendent would somehow exceed even David himself, but this element remains only an implication. The point of the question was to call attention to the scribes' limitations as biblical interpreters and theologians. Indeed, Jesus cited the full verse, in which God promises the descendent of David whom David describes as "my lord" that God will subject the descendant's enemies to him. Mark's Greek has "until I put them under your feet," an adequate paraphrase of the Hebrew "until I make them a footstool for your feet." Anyone familiar with Psalm 110 would have also thought of the continuation of the psalm in which God promises to extend the dominion of the Messiah figure "from Zion . . . in the midst of [his] enemies" (110:2).

Although Jesus did not overtly claim to be the Messiah in this question, the allusions and echoes it invokes are manifold, powerful, and, from the scribal perspective, confrontational. Standing in the temple on Mt. Zion, "in the midst of his enemies," Jesus cited a promise that God would subject the Messiah's enemies to his dominion! Jesus not only exposed the scribes' limited expertise as interpreters of Scripture, then, but also implied that God would give him victory over these enemies, making them footstools for "the lord" seated at God's right hand. Jesus' seemingly academic question was tantamount to a declaration of war against Israel's religious leadership!

The responses to Jesus' question are telling: the scribes remained silent (what could they say?), but the "great crowd heard him gladly." In his denunciation of the scribes as pompous hypocrites and cheats (12:38-40), Jesus stated openly the implications of his rhetorical question. The scribes await "great condemnation." In only a few days, Jesus' enemies would act to rid themselves of this troublemaker who dared challenged their authority, embarrass them publicly, and outwit them at every turn. As so often in human history, the party with the weaker argument but greater political power resorted to force. According to Mark, Jesus' opponents were no match for him in the debate hall, but they could manipulate the legal system as a murder weapon.

Jesus' Battle of Wits with One Sharp Syro-Phoenician Woman

According to Mark, Jesus "lost," as it were, only one exchange of wits, not to a scribe or Pharisee but to a Gentile woman, a Syro-Phoenician. The specifics of the story, recorded in Mark 7:24-30, seem straightforward enough, although its implications for the life and work of Jesus have long puzzled commentators. On this occasion, Jesus had withdrawn from the public eye, as he sometimes did, presumably to rest and pray. Jesus' efforts to remain incognito in a home in Tyre, just north of Israel in Phoenicia (modern Lebanon), did not succeed. A local woman whose daughter was demon-possessed heard of Jesus' presence and came to implore him to heal the girl. Jesus' response to her request represents the difficulty for interpreters. Just as he had responded to his opponents who complained that he associated with sinners, Jesus replied to the woman's request with a witty proverb, "You feed the children first. It is not good to take the children's food and throw it to the dogs" (7:27, my translation). Did Jesus mean to compare the Gentile woman to a dog in a derogatory fashion, suggesting that he saw himself as the Messiah for the Jews only? Was Jesus' understanding of his mission still developing such that he had not yet come to realize the place for Gentiles in the kingdom of God? Did Jesus envision a Gentile mission, but only after Easter, so that he regarded the woman's request to be premature? None of these possibilities conforms well to the fact that, according to Mark (5:1-20), Jesus had already healed the presumably Gentile maniac from Gerasa, in the Decapolis (Jews would not have been swineherds), the region to which Jesus returned after the episode involving the Syro-Phoenician woman (Mark 7:31). Was Jesus simply testing her convictions concerning Jesus' authority, her determination and persistence, her love for her daughter?

Whatever the case may be regarding the motivation for Jesus' initial rebuff, the account clearly reveals the woman's motives and character. From the outset, she demonstrated genuine acceptance of Jesus' authority by "bowing at his feet" (7:25), calling him "Lord," and "entreating" him to exorcise the demon from her daughter (7:26). Unlike Jesus' cynical opponents, this Gentile woman was willing to accept the evidence of Jesus' acts of healing. Furthermore, to the extent that theology involves interpretive skill, she was a much better theologian than Jesus' opponents. While she obviously acknowledged Jesus' authority to heal, however, she was also persistent and, above all, witty in a manner that was simultaneously bold and humble. With debate skills far exceeding those of Jesus' opponents, in a spontaneous retort of the first caliber, she turned Jesus' dogs-at-the-dinner-table scenario to her advantage. She was not presuming to eat from the table, but she argued that there could be no harm in permitting her the crumbs that fall to the floor.

We may not be able to discern with any confidence what motivated Jesus initially to refuse the woman's request, but his reaction to her rejoinder is crystal clear. He was impressed. Only she had "bested" him in a challenge of wits. In contrast to the ill will of the scribes, Pharisees, Herodians, and Sadducees whom Jesus outwitted, Jesus could yield graciously when a dialogue partner scored a valid point. She was right: there is plenty of food in the kingdom of God to go around. Even the crumbs are delicacies. Jesus healed the woman's daughter immediately.

Sharp-witted Discipleship

What insights does Jesus' distinctive use of humor yield about our Master and about being his disciples? First, Jesus was obviously a quick wit with a mastery of Scripture and marvelous skill as an interpreter of it. Repeatedly, his opponents attempted to catch him in some violation or misinterpretation of Mosaic law, to squeeze him between popular sentiments and Roman demands, or to construct a hypothetical situation too ridiculous for even Jesus to resolve. Repeatedly, seemingly without hesitation or pause to reflect, Jesus parried their efforts, counterattacked, and forced his enemies into silence or retreat, publicly humiliating them. He was a good debater. Second, along the way, Jesus demonstrated the importance of what one might call "global" interpretation of Scripture. In order to properly understand the Sabbath commandment, for example, Jesus showed that one must not focus solely on the prohibition but also seek to comprehend the impulse of the commandment, namely to nurture and enrich authentic human life before God. Emphasis on the rules, per se, can perversely result in the opposite of their true intent.

While Jesus' skill as a debater and interpreter was remarkable, his technique for dealing with his opponents should not necessarily be regarded as a model for his disciples to emulate, at least not in every situation. In his dealings with the scribes, Pharisees, Sadducees, and Herodians, Jesus was not acting in his role as the Good Shepherd of the flock, but as reproachful teacher or indignant prophet. Alternatively, one could argue that Jesus, the Good Shepherd, treated his opponents as wolves among the sheep, the audience of everyday people to whom Jesus appealed. Clearly, as Mark relates events, Jesus' behavior toward his opponents became increasingly aggressive. He did not attempt to placate his enemies. Instead, he confronted them, challenged them, uncovered the weaknesses in their arguments, and even exposed them to public ridicule. Of course, he did so because they seemed determined *not* to consider the possibility that Jesus might be right or that his ministry, like John's, had its foundation in divine authority. Jesus recognized this obstinacy early on, according to Mark, and crafted his communication strategy to address the public, his true flock, the audience that gathered to see him heal and hear him teach—and to hear him dumbfound his obdurate opposition. Jesus wisely understood that these opponents could not be persuaded because they would not allow themselves to be, so he apparently abandoned the effort, choosing instead to make object lessons of them. Just as Jesus taught in parables so that those with ears might hear, he refuted his enemies not to instruct them but to teach his audience. Mark included these accounts for the same reasons—not to condemn Jews, Judaism, or its religious leadership but to invite his readers to amazement at Jesus' skill and, above all, to encourage them to *listen* to his teaching.

In the end, of course, Jesus' treatment of his enemies only hardened their resolve to destroy him, but evidently nothing short of Jesus' abandoning his mission would have satisfied them. Jesus could not be silent. The incongruity here gives pause. "What would Jesus do?" may not always be the question for his disciples to ask themselves—at least not if his disciples seek a comfortable, comforting answer. Jesus would side with the poor and would confront the privileged, the powerful, and the prideful, even to the point of provoking anger; Jesus would focus on authentic living and anything that nurtures it. Ironically, to read Mark's account of Jesus' debates today raises the question of whether we are more like the scribes and Pharisees or the audience, amazed and delighted at Jesus' audacity. "Gentle Jesus, Meek and Mild" indeed!

Notes

1. Luke 6:11 softens the opponents' reaction somewhat.

2. With the exception of Matthew's placement of the question concerning the greatest commandment (Matt 10:25-28), both Matthew and Luke preserve Mark's sequence of Jesus' disputations with the Jewish religious leadership. Matthew differs from Mark (and Luke) in delaying the first of these disputations until much later in his account of Jesus' ministry (Matt 9:14-17).

Chapter 6

Peter and Cornelius

"Laugh at yourself first, before anyone else can."
(Elsa Maxwell)

People frequently say to me, "You're an Old Testament professor. You may find humor in the Old Testament, but the New Testament tells the gospel story and that's just not funny." In fact, however, since the New Testament tells the gospel story as it involves *people*—the apostles, the scribes and Pharisees, members of the early church, Paul and people in Paul's circle—and since people are invariably humorous, it would be odd if there were no humor *even in the New Testament*. Indeed, in this chapter, we will examine the first subsection of the book of Acts that tells the story of the early church as it tries to come to grips with what it is to be God's people in the world between the life and ministry of Jesus and the full coming of the kingdom of God. In other words, it recounts the life and work of the early church in the new setting of tension between the kingdom of God in our midst and the kingdom to come, between the now and the not-yet—in short, in a situation that is inherently and fundamentally incongruous.

When we read the New Testament, we typically focus our attention, of course, on the main character, Jesus. A whole cast of figures surrounds him, however. We can expect that people like you and me—and the early church was full of people like you and me—will sometimes do incongruous things in such an inherently incongruous context. We can also expect, therefore, that the humor we may encounter in the book of Acts will involve characterization, not the acerbic wit of Jesus battling for the hearts and minds of his audience. As far as I can tell, there are no jokes with punch lines either. Furthermore, in contrast to the Old Testament, plays on words seem to be rare. Instead, we see normal, fallible people trying to come to grips with the enormity of what God has done in and through Christ Jesus. Being the finite and fallible creatures that they were, and that we are, the task sometimes surpassed their abilities as it sometimes exceeds ours. To see the people in the early church struggling to understand what God is up to in the world, even when the evidence is overwhelming and obvious, calls to mind a period in my youth when, like many preteens and teenagers, my powers of sustained observation were not well developed—when I was very absent-minded. Sent to fetch something from a closet or a pantry, but unable to find it because my mind was everywhere else, I would announce that it was not there. Mother, of course, found it immediately because it was right in front of me. "If it had been a snake," she would say, "it would have bit you." The book of Acts begins by recounting how Jesus had departed and left behind the cast of those who had surrounded him during his earthly ministry. It will immediately become evident to us that the task with which Jesus commissioned the early church was right in front of them even though they were slow to see it. *If it had been a snake . . .*

The Church's Mission: God's Plan in the Hands of Shortsighted People

We will look closely at a couple of passages, but first let's set the context from the beginning of the book of Acts, where we find a significant clue about the attitudes of the disciples in the earliest period of the church. In the account of the ascension of Jesus after the resurrection, we read one of the great texts about the mission of the church in the world, arguably the thesis statement of the book of Acts:

> So when they had come together, they asked him, "Lord, is this the time when you will restore the kingdom to Israel?" He replied, "It is not for you to know the times or periods that the Father has set by his own authority. But you will receive power when the Holy Spirit has come upon you. And you will be my witnesses in Jerusalem, in all Judea and Samaria, and to the ends of the earth." (Acts 1:6, RSV)

This text reveals the two perspectives involved in the discussion between Jesus and his disciples, and ultimately reflected in the growth of the early church. Have you ever noticed the question the disciples asked Jesus? They asked, "Lord, is this the time when you will restore the *kingdom* to *Israel?*" From the standpoint of the apostles, the disciples, and the early church, surely the next step after Jesus' crucifixion and resurrection was to be the restoration of the Davidic kingdom and the rise of Israel to the place of prominence it deserved in the world. Rome would fall from power; the Gentile occupation of Israel would end. The tables would be turned. Incidentally, the disciples probably expected to receive positions of power and authority in Jesus' government. Notably, Jesus' response simply avoided all these matters: "No, I want you to stay here until you receive power, and in that power that you will receive from the Holy Spirit you will be my witnesses." Where? In Jerusalem, to be sure, and in Judea, but also in Samaria and ultimately to the whole world. The disciples hoped for the power to *exert dominance over the world*; Jesus promised them the power to *bear witness to the world*. As we know from all four of the Gospels, this *incongruity* between the purposes of Jesus and the understanding of the disciples was nothing new.

Mark reports three instances, beginning at Caesarea Philippi just after Peter's great confession (Mark 8:29), when Jesus taught his disciples that "the Son of Man must undergo great suffering, and be rejected by the elders, the chief priests, and the scribes, and be killed, and after three days rise again" (8:31). In fact, as Mark stresses ("He said all this quite openly," 8:32a), Jesus taught this idea explicitly, not in parables as he often taught, presumably because he wanted to enhance the possibility that his disciples would understand. It did not work. The disciples had their own notions concerning the nature of Jesus' mission and ministry. After confessing Jesus as his *Messiah*, his Lord, Peter responded to Jesus' teaching about the coming passion and resurrection by *rebuking* Jesus for daring to express foolish notions about suffering, rejection, and death (Mark 8:32b)! For Peter, the coming of the Messiah could only mean the restoration of the Davidic monarchy. Even though he had been with Jesus throughout Jesus' earthly ministry, he could not see past his own expectations. *If it had been a snake . . .*

After witnessing Jesus' transfiguration and the healing of the mute boy, and just after the second instance when Jesus openly predicted his coming passion, Mark reports that the disciples "did not understand what he was saying, and they were afraid to ask him" (9:32). In fact, Jesus caught them in an argument among themselves concerning which of them was the greatest (Mark 9:34)! Clearly, they had tunnel vision focused on restoring a political kingdom, on coming to political power, on their own status and authority. On the way to Jerusalem for the final week of Jesus' life, after he reiterated the "Passion Prediction," as scholars call it, James and John (Matt 20:20 says it was their mother!) boldly, even impudently, asked Jesus to "do for [them] whatever they asked" (Mark 10:35)! In the context of Jesus' prediction of his coming suffering and death, the irony of their specific request that they be granted the privilege of sitting "one at [his] right hand and one at [his] left, in [his] glory" (Mark 10:37) only highlights their fixation on their own plans. They knew not what they asked. James and John could have been crucified alongside the middle cross!

From our perspective, we consider the events that transpired in this brief time—Jesus' crucifixion and resurrection three days later and the gift of the Holy Spirit almost fifty days after that—to be life changing and of worldwide significance. We understand that these events simply cannot affect only a local population of people. If the Lord were to raise someone from the dead in Richmond, (I hope that) Christians in Richmond would not think, "Okay, let's make sure all of Richmond knows about it, but let's not tell anybody in Ashland. We don't want them to find out. We certainly don't want those folks down there in North Carolina to know. And, by all means, let's keep the Yankees from ever knowing anything about it, because they don't deserve to know!"

Provincial Prejudice?

Apparently, however, the early church thought just that, as evidenced not only by their interest in domination and political power but also by their behaviors. We will focus attention on Peter, the first of the apostles. It is interesting to note that, beginning with Peter's speech at Pentecost and for the several occasions thereafter, Peter addressed only Israelites: "Oh, fellow Israelites." He thought of the good news as a local phenomenon. God had raised Jesus from the dead, but Peter did not recognize that the whole world needed to hear this news. *If it had been a snake* . . . This constricted, parochial view of the gospel was so much a problem for the early church that we read about it in an episode (Acts 6) often celebrated as the foundation of the diaconate (the establishment of deacons as servants of the church). If we pay attention to certain details of the account, however, another, much less positive theme emerges pointing to the shortsightedness of early church leaders like Peter.

"Now during those days, when the disciples were increasing in number, the Hellenists complained against the Hebrews because their widows were being neglected in the daily distribution of food" (Acts 6:1). The terms used here to describe the two groups of people involved can be confusing. The Hellenists would have been Jewish people who were not born in Israel but who had come back to Jerusalem for whatever reason and had now become followers of Jesus. The Jerusalem church, then, included a significant population of transplanted Jewish Christian widow women on one hand and of native Jewish Christian widow women on the other. Commendably, the apostles took regular and active care of the needy in the church. It so happened, however, that when they went about on their daily rounds, they would always go first to the local Jewish Christian widow women, so that by the time they had gotten around to the returned Jewish Christian widow women, the bread was already gone. This pattern repeated itself every day. The apostles naturally favored people who, like themselves, were born in the land of Israel, but they believed in a gospel destined to bring the news of the kingdom of God to the whole world, without distinction, and certainly without favoritism. *If it had been a snake* . . . . What does this brief report tell us about the attitudes of the early apostles? Did they actively conspire against Jewish-Christian immigrants, or were their habits just an expression of what they thought of as a natural behavior? One takes care of one's own kind first, right? Remarkably, both groups consisted of Jewish widows who had become followers of Jesus Christ. Apparently, however, perhaps subconsciously, the apostles saw only the women born in Israel, the "Hebrews," as "their own."

Does this situation imply that the apostles were prejudiced against the Greeks, even against Jews who spoke Greek? If they distinguished between Jewish-Christian widows based solely on their birthplaces (and accents?), treating newcomers as second class, were they going to be eager, even open, to the idea of the gospel spreading "to Samaria and the ends of the earth"? Would they rush to bring the good news to the despised "half-Jewish" Samaritans? What would they think about Gentiles following Jesus? Everyone knows this phenomenon intimately. It is common in my southern Appalachian hometown. There, when you meet someone you do not know personally, you start out by exploring whether your granddaddy knew their granddaddy. If your granddaddy knew their granddaddy, then they are potentially okay. At least they will know how to behave. As to the details, you can find out everything you want to know about your new acquaintance—whether they are trustworthy, the kind of people they are, the kind of people *their* people are—as soon as you have a chance to talk to your mother. *"I ran into So-and-So today at the barbershop. He's Such-and-Such's grandson. He wanted to know if I would go in with him and buy a cow. What should I do?"* If your family did not have deep roots in my hometown, people did not mistreat you, but they certainly did not trust you without good reason.

A Solution that Foreshadows Events to Come

Returning from the Appalachian South to first-century Jerusalem, we find a group of Christian widows who have moved into town from abroad. Now,

I am sure that Peter would have agreed that the church should care for its needy, regardless of their place of birth. Yet neither he nor the other apostles thought that caring for them was a top priority. Every day they were last on the list. Ultimately, the Hellenistic widows complained. Therefore,

> the twelve called together the whole community of the disciples and said, "It is not right that we should neglect the word of God in order to wait at tables. Therefore, friends, select from among yourselves seven men of good standing, full of the Spirit and of wisdom, whom we may appoint to this task, while we, for our part, will devote ourselves to prayer and to serving the word." (Acts 6:2, NRSV)

To paraphrase, the twelve apostles—the disciples who had heard Jesus say that to be greatest of all is to be servant of all, who had watched as Jesus washed the feet of eleven of the twelve (now minus Judas, of course)—responded, *"Well, we're ministers of the gospel. We need to be praying and studying, and these sorts of menial tasks of taking care of people—we can't be bothered with them."* They seem to have implied that if they had been falling short in some way, it was because they should not have had to trouble themselves with caring for the needy in the first place! They could not see the need in front of them because their minds were on higher things. What could be higher, however, than caring for "one of the least," since doing so is nothing less than caring for Jesus himself (Matt 25:31-46)? *If it had been a snake . . . .* It is good to remember that the apostles were ordinary people whom Jesus had called to do the extraordinary. Apparently, they still had room to grow.

"What they said pleased the whole community, and they chose" six men, perhaps as the church's first "deacons" (the word derives from the Greek *diakoneo*, "to wait tables"). The first deacons delivered "meals on wheels"—actually probably "dinners on donkeys"—to widows. Apart from the humble service that characterized the work of the first deacons, perhaps the most interesting aspect of this episode involves whom the Jerusalem church chose for the duty and what their names were: "Stephen, a man full of faith and the Holy Spirit, together with Philip, Prochorus, Nicanor, Timon, Parmenas" (Acts 6:5). These are all Greek names. In other words, when the community had a chance to select the people who would see to it that both native-born and returned widows were cared for equally, whom did they choose? All Hellenistic Jewish Christian men, including even "Nicolaus, a proselyte." He, too, was a Hellenistic Jewish Christian, but he was a convert to Judaism rather than a native-born Jew with Jewish parents. Ethnically, he was Greek, a Gentile, as far as we know, the first Gentile leader in the Christian church. Furthermore, Stephen, who had a Greek name, was the first recorded Christian martyr (Acts 7:54-60), and Philip, who also had a Greek name, shared the gospel message with the Ethiopian eunuch (Acts 8:26-39).

Without the apostles' authorization, without even their knowledge, this Philip first boldly preached the gospel in Samaria to the *Samaritans* (Acts 8:5-8)! The apostles only sent John and Peter up to see whether Philip's work among the Samaritans was acceptable after the fact. The more things change, the more they stay the same (Acts 8:14). Since the beginning, apparently, when something unexpected or extraordinary happens, the church has gathered together a commission and sent it off to investigate and make recommendations. This instance is truly remarkable. Peter and John, no less, arrived in Samaria where the gospel had been preached. *Samaritans* had believed in Jesus; *Samaritans* had been baptized; *Samaritans* had received the Holy Spirit. It sounds as though Philip and, more importantly, God already had things under control, but Peter and John had to pronounce it acceptable. What else were they going to say?

Phillip went down, on instructions from the Holy Spirit, to the road that runs down to the south and encountered the Ethiopian eunuch, who was reading, as it happened, from the book of Isaiah. The context implies, at least, that he was reading Isaiah 56, which addresses two issues particularly pertinent to an Ethiopian eunuch. It says that eunuchs will one day have a memorial in the temple of God that will be better than sons and daughters. Isaiah 56 also invites the foreigner who wants join in the worship of the Lord to come right on into the temple. In other words, Isaiah 56 speaks against excluding foreigners, non-Israelites, from temple worship. In it, God proclaims, "My house will be called a house of prayer for all people," a promise Jesus quoted when he cleansed the temple, by the way. Thus, led by the Spirit, Philip went to an Ethiopian, a foreigner, who was, furthermore, a eunuch. When he found him reading the gospel in Isaiah, Philip interpreted it to him in relation to salvation in Jesus, and then he baptized him.

A Church Slow to Understand

Someone has said that the book of Acts ought not to be called the Acts of the Apostles because they do very little on their own initiative with the clear intention of fulfilling Jesus' commission recorded in Acts 1. Jesus had charged them, "Be witnesses to the whole world. Start at home and work your way outward." Yet they did not set about making plans to spread the gospel. They started by electing someone to take Judas's place. They went fishing. They hid in upper rooms. They took bold new steps only by accident, or what seems like an accident, or, more precisely, because the Spirit of God engineered a situation in which they virtually had to do what God wanted them to do in the first place. Peter did not preach the gospel until the Holy Spirit fell on the church and he found it necessary to explain what had happened to bystanders. In fact, judging from the way they treated the Hellenistic Jewish Christian widows and their reaction to the Samaritan mission, the apostles were not eager to see the gospel spread to the whole world. They had difficulty with the notion that Samaritans, who, in their view, were half-Jews, could believe. The idea of flat-out Gentiles becoming followers of Jesus had not crossed their minds. Given their cultural conditioning perhaps, it could not. *If it had been a snake . . .*

One of my preaching professors used to tell his students that when you read the biblical story one of the questions you should ask is, "Who am I in this story?" Well, in the story we have heard so far, I am certainly not the Holy Spirit or Jesus. I am not the angel. As I narrow the possibilities, it is beginning to look bad for me. Either I am most like one of the neglected, even discounted widows, eunuchs, or Samaritans, or I am like Peter and John, slow to understand the full implications of the gospel, slow to reach out to people different from me, and suspicious of those who do so. One might expect that the leadership of the early church would surely soon catch on to what the Holy Spirit was doing in the world. Unfortunately, one could argue that even today the church still has not caught on fully to what God is obviously doing in the world. Saved by God's grace, incongruously, the church is still surprised to discover God's grace at work abroad in the world. *If it were a snake . . .*

Simon Peter at the Tanner's House

Now that we have an idea of the cultural dynamics and, dare we say, prejudices at work in the early church, we are prepared to "get it" when we read the story of Peter and the Roman centurion, Cornelius. "In Caesarea there was a man named Cornelius, a centurion of the Italian Cohort, as it was called. He was a devout man who feared God with all his household; he gave alms generously to the people and prayed constantly to God" (Acts 10:1-2, NRSV).

As the Bible so often does and does well, it conveys a wealth of information in this brief introduction. Judging from his name and his military affiliation, Cornelius was a native-born Roman from the Italian peninsula, not some outlying province—a real Roman. He was an officer, accustomed to command, in the army that occupied Peter's Israel. On the other hand, he seems to have belonged among those Gentiles who revered the God of Israel, although they did not go as far as converting. He, his family, and his servants all "feared God." They even practiced two of what the rabbis called the "three notable duties" (prayer, fasting, and almsgiving). The rabbinical literature calls such people "righteous Gentiles" and discourages their conversion to Judaism since, it argues, God will honor their righteous faith. They can gain no advantage by also shouldering the covenant responsibilities incumbent on Israel. Evidence from the first century suggests that such God-fearers could be found throughout the empire.

Now that we know the who, the account can move on to the what:

> One afternoon at about three o'clock he had a vision in which he clearly saw an angel of God coming in and saying to him, "Cornelius." He stared at him in terror and said, "What is it, Lord?" He answered, "Your prayers and your alms have ascended as a memorial before God. Now send men to Joppa for a certain Simon who is called Peter; he is lodging with Simon, a tanner, whose house is by the seaside." (Acts 10:3-6, NRSV)

This brief statement also contains a lot of information that we need to unpack. First, God sent an angelic messenger to Cornelius to announce that God had noticed him. In fact, God's message alludes to the Isaiah 56 passage mentioned earlier, a passage that promises "a memorial" to those previously excluded from worshiping God in the temple. In other words, Cornelius did not take the initiative on his own accord. He did not think, *What am I going to do to get to know the gospel? I think I'll send for Peter.* He did not know that he needed to hear the gospel, and he had probably never heard of Peter. After all, those who need to hear aren't responsible to arrange for a preacher; the church, sent by God, is to go into the world to preach so that those who need the gospel may hear it. Despite Jesus' commission to bear witness to the uttermost parts of the earth, Peter did not take the initiative either. We do not read anywhere about Peter deliberating and planning an approach to a worldwide mission. The Bible does not record Peter thinking or saying, *In a strategy of evangelizing the world, if we want to get the good news out to the Gentiles, a good place to start would be with the God-fearers right here at home. I'll find someone who is prominent in that community and begin with him.* Understandably, Cornelius was clueless on his own of his need to hear the gospel, but, astonishingly, Peter was equally blind to the opportunity for spreading the gospel to those represented by God-fearing Roman centurions like Cornelius! *If it had been a snake* . . . God had to send a vision to Cornelius because, apart from events such as the bold impetus of the Holy Spirit transporting Philip to the Ethiopian eunuch and guiding Cornelius, the church would have apparently remained an obscure sect of Palestinian Judaism.

Second, the text refers to two people named "Simon"—Simon Peter, our Simon, and an otherwise unknown Simon, a tanner by trade. Significantly, the tanner's trade, which involved handling the hides of dead animals, was unclean by definition under Jewish purity laws, the same laws Simon Peter would later claim to have observed assiduously. Yet our Simon Peter was staying at the home of this tanner and eating food at his table prepared in his kitchen. I wonder whether Simon Peter recognized the ironic "incongruity" (or hypocrisy?) between his claim and his behavior. Now that we have noted the basic incongruity inherent in the situation from the outset, it will be interesting to see how events unfold.

> When the angel who spoke to him [Cornelius] had left, he called two of his slaves and a devout soldier from the ranks of those who served him, and after telling them everything, he sent them to Joppa. About noon the next day, as they were on their journey and approaching the city, Peter went up on the roof to pray. He became hungry and wanted something to eat; and while it was being prepared, he fell into a trance. He saw the heaven opened and something like a large sheet coming down, being lowered to the ground by its four corners. In it were all kinds of four-footed creatures and reptiles and birds of the air. Then he heard a voice saying, "Get up, Peter; kill and eat." But Peter said, "By no means, Lord; for I have never eaten anything that is profane or unclean." (Acts 10:7-14, NRSV)

Who was Peter trying to kid? If he ate the meal being prepared even as he spoke with God in this trance, if he ate anything prepared in the house of Simon the tanner, it would be as unclean as a bacon cheeseburger! Simon the tanner was unclean. The bed Simon Peter had slept in that night was unclean. The roof on which he was sitting and praying was unclean. Everything within reach was unclean. Judging by his name, we can assume that Simon the tanner was a Jew, a Jewish Christian no doubt. Peter overlooked Greek-speaking Jewish widows, he doubted the mission to "half" Jewish

Samaritans, and he claimed to observe kosher food regulations, but he was lodging and eating with a tanner. *If it had been a snake* . . . Peter may have been fooling himself, but he certainly was not fooling God. Could there be any significance in the fact that, just as Peter had denied Jesus three times and Jesus thrice asked him, "Do you love me?" Peter insisted on his absolute observance of purity laws three times (Acts 10:16)?

> Now while Peter was greatly puzzled about what to make of the vision that he had seen, suddenly the men sent by Cornelius appeared. They were asking for Simon's house and were standing by the gate. They called out to ask whether Simon, who was called Peter, was staying there. While Peter was still thinking about the vision, the Spirit said to him, "Look, three men are searching for you. Now get up, go down, and go with them without hesitation; for I have sent them." So Peter went down to the men and said, "I am the one you are looking for; what is the reason for your coming?" They answered, "Cornelius, a centurion, an upright and God-fearing man, who is well spoken of by the whole Jewish nation, was directed by a holy angel to send for you to come to his house and to hear what you have to say." (Acts 10:17-22, NRSV)

God, the Holy Spirit, was rather busy coordinating this scenario, sending an angel to Cornelius and timing Peter's vision so that it took place just as Cornelius's messengers arrived at Simon's door. How else would Peter have come to realize that the gospel of Jesus Christ's crucifixion and resurrection was good news for Roman centurions, too? Obviously, these visions were the New Testament equivalent of an object lesson. The point was not, as people often assume, to invalidate the Old Testament's kosher rules. There are other texts and other reasons dealing with why Gentile Christians are not required to keep kosher. Most prominently, the leadership of the early church decided that question later on at the so-called "Jerusalem Council" (Acts 15), after Paul had begun his missionary work among Gentiles. On occasion, in fact, Peter kept kosher in regard to eating together with Gentile Christians, which was, according to Paul, an act of hypocrisy and cowardice (Gal 2:11-14). Many Jewish Christians today still observe purity requirements, not because they think it is necessary to do so for their salvation but because they still honor their Jewish identity. No, the point lies in God's assertion that whatever God pronounced clean, Peter must not regard otherwise. God made the kosher rules; God can stipulate the exceptions. The question is whether Peter got the point. Would Peter behave as he had when

Jesus foretold his Passion? Would Peter "rebuke" God for speaking such fool-ishness, for teaching contrary to Peter's longstanding expectations? Would Peter be able to see what was right in front of him?

Peter's initial reaction to the men standing at the door is promising, at least. He invited them in and gave them lodging for the night instead of turning them away because they were Gentiles—Romans, in fact. Moreover, they rose the next morning and went together to Cornelius's house. But the next event in the story is absolutely, staggeringly amazing.

Peter at the Centurion's House

> On Peter's arrival Cornelius met him, and falling at his feet, worshipped him. But Peter made him get up, saying, "Stand up; I am only a mortal." And as he talked with him, he went in and found that many had assem-bled; and he said to them, "You yourselves know that it is unlawful for a Jew to associate with or to visit a Gentile; but God has shown me that I should not call anyone profane or unclean. So when I was sent for I came without objection. Now may I ask why you sent for me?" (Acts 10:25-29, NRSV)

"Why did you send for me?" Let's see, why would someone send for Peter, the preacher of the first Christian sermon ever at Pentecost? Did he think that they wanted him to take them fishing? If we were to invite Billy Graham to join us Easter Sunday morning, I should think that we would not have to specify that we are inviting him to preach. Paul McCartney knows that people expect him to sing; he is a singer. Politicians give speeches. Comedians tell jokes. Peter was a preacher, perhaps the most prominent preacher in the early church—indeed, the acknowledged leader of the Jerusalem church. He was Pentecost Peter. He was the Peter who had been before the Sanhedrin boldly bearing witness to his faith. He had chaired the commission sent to investigate whether the Samaritans had received the gospel. Yet, after all the effort God had gone through, Peter stood at the door looking at this assembly gathered to hear him preach the gospel with-out a clue as to why Cornelius wanted to see him. They had probably borrowed all the neighbors' folding chairs, as it were, and arranged them to accommodate the whole household, and probably some of the neighbors, maybe even some of the Roman soldiers under Cornelius's command. They had placed a makeshift lectern or a comfortable chair at the front of the room. Everyone was seated, expectant. Peter the preacher, whom God told

Cornelius to send for, had arrived only to say, incredulously, *"I'm here. What do you want with me?"* Poor Peter. *If it had been a snake . . .*

We want you not to be so slow, Peter. That's what we want of you. You're a little thick, my friend. Of course, Peter had always been a bit clueless. We remember the episode in which he walked on water for a little while. We remember Peter arguing with James and John about which disciple would be Jesus' deputy. We remember Peter at Caesarea Philippi confessing that Jesus is the Son of God, his Lord, only to rebuke Jesus a moment later, insisting that Jesus had it all wrong about the crucifixion and the resurrection. Jesus recognized the temptation presented by Peter's insistence that there was no need to suffer. Jesus even called Peter, "the Rock" whose faith would be the foundation of the church, "Satan, the Accuser." We remember Peter, so quick to promise steadfast loyalty, denying Jesus three times in succession. We remember Peter virtually giving up shortly after the first Easter and going back to what he knew best, fishing.

How many times would Peter fail to see who Jesus is and what Jesus' life and death mean? Clearly, he had not yet fully understood and certainly had not wholeheartedly embraced the commission Jesus gave all the way back in Acts 1. It was not native to his background and identity to think about the ends of the earth. He was a Galilean fisherman. In context, he was also something of a buffoon—trying to dictate how his Lord and Master would behave, conveniently overlooking Hellenistic widows, unable to recognize an opportunity to proclaim the gospel to a waiting and willing audience. Where was Peter's mind? Could he see what was right in front of him? As I read this story, it seems that the light did not go on all at once for Peter. His light was on a dimmer switch. First, he learned that God would determine clean and unclean, so he accepted the messengers from Cornelius and even accompanied them to Cornelius's house because he had learned that "God is no respecter of persons." Even then, however, he did not understand the implications of what he had just said, namely that the gospel is also available to everyone. *"Okay, God said I have to go with you, so I'll go with you even though I don't see why. . . . All right, I'm here. What do you want?"* Cornelius said, *"Four days ago I was praying and I had this vision, and it said to send for you and so I sent for you, and now you're here. What we'd like to know, what we'd like to hear, is the gospel message."*

Therefore, Peter began to tell the gospel story, rather begrudgingly, by the way, and very briefly. In many ways, Peter resembled the Old Testament prophet Jonah discussed in an earlier chapter of this book. When Jonah finally went to Nineveh to preach, he preached a sermon of only five words in Hebrew: "Forty days until things change." Since Peter was willing to preach the gospel, maybe he had finally caught on to what God was up to in the world. Or so one might think. To be safe, though, just as with Jonah and the Ninevites, God did not want to depend on the clarity and efficacy of Peter's preaching.

> While Peter was still speaking, the Holy Spirit fell upon all who heard the word. The circumcised believers who had come with Peter were astounded that the gift of the Holy Spirit had been poured out even on the Gentiles, for they heard them speaking in tongues and extolling God. Then Peter said, "Can anyone withhold the water for baptizing these people who have received the Holy Spirit just as we have?" (Acts 10:44-47)

Peter: Prototype for Today's Church?

Peter constitutes a prime example of how thickheaded any one of us can be because of our expectations and prejudices. The book of Acts as the history of the earliest church describes an extended pattern of behavior. In it, the church eventually took the gospel without fetter to everyone only because the Holy Spirit of God kept pushing the church in that direction, not because the church understood and embraced the message and mission that Jesus gave them any better than Peter did. As a matter of fact, this pattern has continued down through the centuries. Being the proud Southerner that I am, I must nonetheless confess that I belong to a tradition that has recently borne testimony to the continuation of that pattern as well as anybody could. I can almost hear a reader objecting, *"What did you just say? We are not as shortsighted, as xenophobic, as prejudiced as Peter was. How can you imply that we are as slow to understand as he was?"*

I will be more explicit. I said that the church in the South in the 1950s and the 1960s behaved just like Peter and worse. We could sing the hymns about God coming to save everyone and about Jesus loving "red and yellow, black and white," we could quote the statement in Ephesians (4:4-6) that there is "one Spirit . . . one Lord, one faith, one baptism, one God and Father of all," and we could quote Paul's rhapsodic assertion that "in Christ there is neither Jew nor Greek, slave nor free, male nor female" (Gal 3:28) while still making distinctions between people as though there were categories and classes in the kingdom of God. *If it had been a snake . . .* At least in my understanding of history, I am sorry to say that I cannot point to a time when the church has uniformly taken the lead in changing society and its structures in ways that recognize that God shows no partiality. We have been like Peter, Stephen, Philip, and even Paul, in that the Holy Spirit of God, God at work in the world, is far out ahead of the church, with the church too often resisting God's direction. Has that not been true in our lifetimes, especially in the civil rights movement? Like Peter, we come along after the fact and acknowledge that, since the Spirit of God has fallen on some group of people or some situation in society, we are going to have to accept things.

It may be that we find it difficult to see the humor in Peter's visit to Cornelius because Peter is—and by extension, we are—the buffoon(s) in this situation comedy. This suspicion makes us uncomfortable. It is important to remember that humor has the capacity to show us the truth about ourselves. It involves a truth-telling component. Even if we can laugh about Peter's thick-headedness because that was 2,000 years ago and because it involved Hellenistic Jewish Christian widow women, we are most comfortable distancing ourselves from Peter. We do not know any such people. For us, they are only literary figures, characters in an old story. Perhaps we can shake our heads and chuckle about how gradually Peter upped the dimmer switch without recognizing that the account tells the truth about us, too. On the other hand, I can modernize this story by applying it to some people or some category of people in our world and become controversial very quickly. Instead, let me just say that as I understand the message of the Bible, as I understand the gospel message, God loves everyone. Period. Full stop. No need to go further. That covers it. That is the gospel. If it has taken 2,000 years for us to get that point into our heads, to learn that, then no wonder we laugh at Peter; we are actually laughing at our own folly, our own clownish incongruity.

Peter had to accept a new way of viewing the world and a new understanding of his own place in it. He had to admit that God could love a Roman centurion as much as a Jewish disciple. We can extrapolate that being a follower of Christ means taking a journey to a new place and that all of our lives should be that kind of journey. We can take comfort from the David story, the Isaac story, and even the Peter story. Peter was a buffoon, Isaac was a mama's boy, and David was a scoundrel, but none of that kept God from using them for God's purpose, from moving into a new way, from guiding them to do the work of God in the world. A great deal can be said for having the courage to step forward into God's new future, for turning the lights all the way up and seeing what God is doing, for risking ourselves on God's way.

Chapter 7

Humor in the Bible and the Life of Faith

"Mirth is God's medicine. Everybody ought to bathe in it." (Henry Ward Beecher)

"What soap is to the body, laughter is to the soul." (Yiddish Proverb)

As promised in the introduction, this brief examination of humor in the Bible concludes with a few remarks concerning the significance of the fact that the Bible contains humor and also with several recommendations concerning the tools and approaches that can help facilitate a reader's recognition of humor in the Bible. The observations on the importance of the presence of humor in the Bible fall into two categories. The first involves several comments regarding the nature and function of the Bible as a collection of written communications and, by extension, on the process of communicating the message of God's grace, of bearing witness. The second deals more fundamentally with the theological dimensions of humor and the comic. Together, these two categories of observations and reflections point to the value that the comic contributes to the life of faith and suggest that mature faith and a developed sense of humor complement one another.

Humor and Communication

Theoretically, perhaps, if the Bible contained God's direct pronouncements to humanity detailing the regulations for worship and ethics—that is, if it were a rulebook—it might be devoid of humor. Instead, however, it consists of a collection of writings in a variety of genres composed individually over a span of time encompassing at least a millennium. Moreover, these documents were written in three ancient, now-dead languages. These books relate the story of a family, a nation, and a church and document the history, hymns and prayers, proverbial wisdom, exchanges of correspondence, and prophetic preaching of these people—and more. In short, the Bible contains the record of the experience of specific people in relationship with God. Thus, in a fashion analogous to the incarnation of God's Word, both fully divine and fully human, the Bible encompasses elements of both the divine and the human.

Consequently, it should come as no surprise that the Bible attests to the full range of human emotion and experience: anger, betrayal, compassion, despair, elation, fear, grief, and humor. Too often, people regard the Bible with the one-sided expectation that they will find in it the divine word only. When they do so, they risk mistaking the human for the divine. Specifically, they risk leveling or flattening the relational aspects of the biblical story. They risk mishearing the genuinely human voices in the text. In other words, they risk failing to take seriously Abraham's anguish the night *before* the journey to Mt. Moriah and Isaac's fear when they arrive, or Jesus' agony in Gethsemane. At the other end of the spectrum of human nature, they also risk robbing biblical figures of their comic humanity. Like all human beings everywhere and in all times, the people we read about in Scripture were jokesters and wits, fools and clowns, sometimes pitifully overconfident and other times painfully diffident. In short, the people of God we read about in the Bible were, first and fully, human beings like all others. To make them two-dimensional cartoon characters is to rob ourselves of the opportunity of seeing them as fellow human beings and, therefore, of the possibility of appreciating the parallels between their lives of faith and ours. If we cannot laugh with Sarah over Isaac's birth, we cannot laugh over the joyous incongruities in our own lives. If Peter's blindness does not bemuse and befuddle us, it may well be because we are blind to our own blindness!

The human components of the biblical story of God's work in the world also suggest something about how the church can best tell the story of God's continuing work in the world. As we have seen, biblical humor functions in a least three different ways with respect to the relationship between the speaker/author and a dialogue partner and, in some cases, an audience as a third party. Sometimes (with Isaac, Jonah, and Peter, for example), biblical humor functions like my grandmother's humor to "lubricate" the truth with laughter. As Mary Poppins sang, "A spoonful of sugar makes the medicine go down," or as the southern saying goes, "You can catch more flies with honey than with vinegar." Dour Christians pounding home a puritanical Christianity with persistent determination have difficulty speaking convincingly about the joyous good news. Who wants a joyless faith that cannot laugh? Sometimes, of course, biblical humor participates in a prophetic strategy that challenges a status quo and labels the powerful comically ridiculous; Esther is an example. Sometimes the Bible's humor even becomes aggressive, confronting the willfully ignorant and risking animosity and retaliation; Jesus' humor is an example. Humor is a powerful, flexible instrument, but it must be used wisely so that it can be medicine for the sick and not a placebo for the well, words of challenge for the unjust and not of condemnation for the weary.

Theological Dimension of the Comic

To believe is to have a comic vision, a prophetic vision. Faith calls on us both to see the incongruity between what is and what ought to be and to discern the distinction between the surface appearance and the depth reality. The eyes of faith see more than the obvious. They see the potential for change and hints of underlying and surpassing purpose. Thus, the sense of humor is one of the supremely theological senses. One could argue in something of a reverse chain of reasoning, in fact, that since God created human beings in God's image, and since human beings invariably laugh, God too must have a sense of humor. (How else does one explain men's hairlines in the Biddle family?)

A Comic View of Humanity

The universal human awareness of the comic, an awareness that is God's gift, suggests a number of contributions that humor can make to a life of faith. First, the ability to laugh at one's shortcomings and foibles—whether one's thinning hair, one's tin ear, or any other manifestation of the range of human finitude—points in everyday life to God's grace. Apparently, God created human beings with an innate sense of humor. Furthermore, comic incongruity abounds in everyday human life and, evidently, in the stories of the lives of important biblical figures. Simply put, human beings are comic figures. All of us make silly mistakes; all of us have quirks of character and manner. Some of us have odd gaits, some an unusual sneeze, and some enjoy ketchup on grits. (Not me, in case you wonder; Biddle hairline, yes, but no ketchup on grits.)

Unfortunately, many of us have not incorporated a healthy sense of humor into our faith and theology. Our heritage of sober Puritanism and Greek idealism allows no room for a positive appreciation of comic incongruity. Implicit in much of the preaching and teaching of the church is a notion of human "perfection" that negates an appreciation for the incongruity that is being human.

According to the Bible, God created humankind in God's likeness (Gen 1:26-27), a "little lower than angels/God"[1] (Ps 8:5), with "eternity in [their] mind" (Eccl 3:11). At the same time, however, God created humankind (*adam*) from the red clay (*adamah*) and breathed life into the created, who then became a "living being" (Gen 2:7) like the other animal creatures. Dust we are and to dust we return (Gen 3:19). Could anything be more incongruous than the existence of an animated dirtball made in God's image?

This precarious existence between dirt and divinity defines humanity and accounts for the comic character of all our lives. Understood properly, it can be liberating, especially from the oppressive pursuit of perfection. Although Jesus admonished his followers to be perfect/whole/complete (Gk., *teleios*) in love as God is (Matt 6:43-48), the context of Jesus' admonition indicates that he did not contemplate the idea of absolute human perfection. Indeed, the concept of an absolutely "perfect" human being is comically oxymoronic. What would constitute a "perfect" human being? Would this person be male or female? How tall? Right-handed or left? Would he or she sing soprano, alto, or bass? What is the perfect hair or eye color? Would an absolutely perfect human being simultaneously be "perfectly" talented in music, language, and mathematics? How quickly would the absolutely perfect human being run the absolutely perfect mile? Could he or she fly?

The men on all sides of my family are taller and lankier than average. My maternal grandfather wore size 13 AAA shoes. My youngest son wears 14 1/2 B's. When my oldest son was about six, I took him along with a group of honors students to a holiday performance of the ballet *The Nutcracker*. He was enthralled. A few days later, his mother was praising his schoolwork and, as mothers are wont to do, she allowed her praise to evolve into hyperbole: "Son, you are so smart. When you grow up, you can do anything you want." My six-year-old was already a head taller than his peers and familiar enough with the concept of genetics to foresee what the future would probably hold for him (yes, he is taller than any of his predecessors, but, to his chagrin, shorter than his youngest brother). With wisdom and maturity well beyond his six years, he answered his mother matter-of-factly that she was incorrect: "No, Mama," he said, "I can never be a ballet dancer." To this day, the image of my son, at well over six feet and nearly 200 pounds, leaping across the stage amuses me, shall we say. Can you dance the ballet in basketball shoes?

As my son had already intuited at age six, the idea of absolute human perfection is ridiculous on its face, of course. It is a category mistake. In the *created* world, nothing is or can be perfect in absolute terms. In creation, standards of excellence pertain to the degree to which a specimen meets the expectations of its species. One does not evaluate an apple's singing voice. Apples are not supposed to be able to sing, just as animated dirtballs are not supposed to attain absolute perfection. In fact, such overreaching was the primal human error committed in the Garden of Eden in the first place!

In other words, a sense of humor is God's gift that enables us to accept and appreciate our finitude, our human limitations, and to recognize them not as failures or sins but as inherent in our status as creatures created in God's image. It is no sin to be a mama's boy, although it may be a limitation in some cases. My golf game can be quite an entertaining spectacle. It would be pitiful if I aspired to a career in the PGA, but since, as anyone who has ever seen me play—including me—knows, that will never happen, my gargantuan slice does not matter in the grand scheme of things. As a younger man, I was burdened with pride. Now I have a more profound and realistic sense of humor about myself. I can lighten up and enjoy the exercise—and celebrate the occasional drive that lands in the fairway.

Perfectionism stifles our freedom. It prevents us from accepting the genetic and social givens in our lives, from playing the hand we are dealt as well as we can. Absolute perfection is absolutely beyond our reach. Our innate abilities and learned behaviors establish the parameters of our lives. We can sharpen the former through education, training, and practice; we can modify the latter, for better or worse, through self-reflection and decision. In any case, except perhaps for the prejudices and petty biases we sometimes absorb from our families and cultures and uncritically perpetuate, these are not flaws and certainly not sins.

Laughter is sometimes an expression of the recognition of the incongruity of any human aspiration to perfection. It is sometimes the gracious acknowledgment that, although we bear God's image, we are by no means divine. It testifies to the fact that we recognize that we are creatures and not God, that we are limited and will inevitably fail, that, while we may be the wisest of creatures, we are not and cannot be all-wise. Therefore, we should not expect infinitude and all-wisdom of ourselves. We should forgive ourselves for being human. God already has. To be a human being is to be an anecdote waiting to happen. Ask the producers of ABC's *America's Funniest Home Videos*, and be sure to keep the video recorder handy. This human clownishness is not a flaw. The Bible does not describe Sarah's advanced age as a misdeed; it describes the birth of her son as an occasion for outlandish laughter! Who ever heard of such a thing? God loves us—warts, limps, slips-of-the-tongue, pratfalls, bald pates, and all. I am grateful to my great-uncle of the "pretty face" and the balding pate for teaching me that the proper response to such humanity is the grace of laughter. We just take ourselves too seriously sometimes.

The Flip Side: A Comic Vision and Human Tragedy

A fine line distinguishes comedy from tragedy. If comedy involves a recognition of incongruity, then tragedy involves the dangerous *failure* to recognize it. In the best case, readers of the book of Jonah will recognize the incongruity of an Israelite prophet who confesses faith in the God who created land and sea but still seeks to flee God's presence by sailing to Spain. If not, they risk a fate similar to Jonah's. In the best case, readers of Jonah will also recognize the incongruous nature of Jonah's attitudes toward God's willingness to forgive the Ninevites after God had given Jonah himself a second chance, rescued him from the depths, and graciously provided the means to shield him from the sun and wind. Otherwise, readers may not recognize their own tragic selfishness.

The converse of the need to have a sense of humor about one's finitude, frailty, and limitation points, of course, to the fact that much that human beings regard as supremely significant is actually also comic by virtue of being human. It becomes tragic when it goes unrecognized for what it truly is. Empires? Emperors were born naked and helpless, too. Nations? "Seek first the kingdom of God" (cf. Matt 6:23). Wealth? "Fool! This night your soul is required of you; and the things you have prepared, whose will they be?" (Luke 12:20, RSV). Prestige? "You are dust and to dust you shall return" (Gen 3:19). A comic vision, a faithful vision, sees that the emperor has no clothes.

The Gospel Comedy

Finally, if humor involves the recognition of what ought to be or what truly is, then, in essence, the gospel of Jesus Christ is the comedy par excellence! What greater incongruity can there be than that of the Incarnate Word of God hanging on a cross to die? What mere appearance obscures reality more than Jesus entombed in a garden? Old Sarah giving birth brought the joyous laughter of God's grace. Jesus once objected that his opponents seemed unable to discern the proper responses to bad news and good news. He cited a children's saying, "We played the flute for you, and you did not dance; we wailed, and you did not mourn!" (Matt 11:17; Luke 7:32, NRSV). Surely, post-Easter faith should rejoice that in the resurrection of Jesus Christ, God demonstrated definitively that death, which apparently so dominates our experience of the world, does not have the last word.

The gospel tells the story of God's unwillingness to abandon God's creation to the unfolding tragedy humanity set into motion and ever perpetuates. What could be more tragic than humanity's failure to recognize its Lord? Incongruously, although entirely unmerited, "God so loved the world that he sent his only begotten Son" (John 3:16), and "God shows his love for us in that while we were yet sinners Christ died for us" (Rom 5:8). The incongruity of the gospel elicits a joy more profound than mere laughter. Incongruously, God brings new life through the death of the one "through whom all things were made," the one "in (whom) was life" (John 1:3, 4). God did not allow Jesus' execution as though he were a common criminal to become the grandest tragedy. Instead, God converted it into the deepest joy. In Christ, nothing is as it may seem, and all things are made new.

Hints for Reading Humor in the Bible

This book does not purport to be an exhaustive study of humor in the Bible. Instead, it has focused on several sustained, in two cases book-length (Jonah and Esther), examples of sufficient substance to merit a chapter each. Elements of humor abound elsewhere throughout Scripture, from Paul's parental rhetoric in his letter to Philemon, to the quite literally bathroom humor in the story of Ehud, an early Israelite judge (Judg 3:14-30). Israel's prophets, in particular, were prone to moments of biting sarcasm, as in the case of Isaiah's derisive comparison of the people's frustrated lamentation to the cries of a woman who thinks she is labor but only passes gas (Isa 26:17-28)—an image worthy of Monty Python—and to absurd and shocking theatrical displays, as in the cases of Ezekiel publicly (4:9-17) baking his daily bread over a dung fire or making daily excursions outside Jerusalem after digging through its walls (12:4-16).

It may not be possible to catalog every instance of humor in the Bible. I do not claim to have identified all of them, and seriously doubt, in fact, that I have come close to doing so. Therefore, the major objective of the book must be to provide examples and tools so that readers of Scripture can read the Bible themselves with greater sensitivity to its range and depth of expression. To further that objective, I will conclude with a few hints and recommendations for a strategy of reading Scripture with sharper eyes and ears.

First, the names of biblical characters are important, especially in the Old Testament. They often provide clues to important themes. Isaac means "he laughed" (Gen 17:17-18; 18:12-15; 21:6). Jacob's name (Heb., *ya`qob*, which closely resembles words that mean "heel" and "cheat") points to his behavior in his relationships with his brother (when he grabbed Esau's heel in the apparent attempt to prevent Esau from being born first, Gen 25:26; when, true to his name, he "cheated" Esau out of his father's blessing, Gen 27:36), with his father, and with his father-in-law. Later, God gave him the ironic new name, Israel ("he wrestled with God"), to take along with him as he limped away from his contest with God at the Jabbok (Gen 32:22-32). Moses ("to draw out"), who was drawn from the Nile (Exod 2:10), drew water from the well for Zipporah and her sisters in Midian (Exod 2:19), "drew" Israel out of Egypt, and even drew water from rocks in the wilderness (Exod 17:6), once to his disadvantage (Num 20:8-13). One could easily multiply examples of the importance of names as clues to the character and behavior of biblical figures. Often, modern editors supply information concerning the meanings of biblical names in the footnotes or, in study Bibles, in the commentary. A good one-volume Bible dictionary can serve as a wealth of such information. Taking the time to find out the meanings of the names of key figures will greatly enrich one's ability to engage the biblical story.

Second, one should pay attention to the footnotes. A major obstacle to recognizing humor in the Bible—and many other dynamics inherent in the text of Scripture—stems from the fact that puns, wordplay, idiomatic expressions, etc. are virtually impossible to bring over in translation. Many editions of the Bible, regardless of the version, supply important information concerning these and other translation difficulties in the footnotes. Short of learning Hebrew and Greek, these footnotes, although by no means comprehensive, can either explain the issue at hand or, at least, make an English reader aware of a subtlety in the text. In these cases, a good commentary will probably discuss the situation. Curiosity will certainly bring reward to those who pursue an answer.

Third, one should explore the details of ancient life mentioned in the Bible. Modern Americans have little experience with camels, ancient marital customs, or ancient assumptions concerning the role and status of the first-born male, but much of this information, upon which the full appreciation of the dynamics of an ancient account of an ancient culture depends, is available. One can safely assume, for example, that since the narrator of the story of Isaac's marriage to Rebekah took such pains to relate the episode involving the watering of the camels, it is an important component of the story. We may not have personal knowledge of watering camels, but, especially in the Internet era, virtually anyone can spend a few minutes gathering data and making the few calculations to discover the magnitude of Rebekah's task—which she undertook voluntarily and vigorously!

Fourth, one should pay attention to the kinds of plot, characterization, and structure devices one learned to recognize in literature classes in high school and college. While, for believers, the Bible is unique among the world's literature as Holy Scripture, it is nonetheless still literature and employs the techniques of good writing. Attention to how the biblical authors tell their stories, pray their prayers, preach their sermons, etc. will enhance understanding of the humor, the passion, the anguish, and the joy that the authors seek to convey. The Bible is not flat, two-dimensional material. It is alive with the full range of human experience.

Fifth, one should pay attention to the specific genres contained in the Bible. It is not a uniform literary work. It represents, rather, a collection of sixty-six books written at various times, by various people, for various purposes, and in various genres. The rules for reading prophecy differ from those for reading parables. Incidentally, this observation suggests that one probably should not expect to find humor in prayers of lament or contrition, but should not be surprised to find it in biblical narrative or, in its sarcastic form, in the prophets.

Sixth, one should engage in the judicious use of imagination, especially given the pre-modern writer's aversion to relating the internal dialogue of characters or to supplying descriptive detail. Through its silence on the subject, the Isaac story invites the reader to wonder why Isaac was still unmarried so late in life. The David story announces from the outset that things are not as they may seem with regard to the protagonist, but leaves it to the reader to discern when, how, and why this is so. Why would Jonathan suggest the complicated means for signaling David whether he may return safely to Saul's court or should flee for his life? The text does not state Jonathan's reasons other than to make it clear that Jonathan thought such secrecy necessary. It requires little imagination to conclude that Jonathan feared that his father might have him tailed and that he did not want to lead Saul to David's hiding place. Without the reader's imagination in such cases, the biblical accounts often remain flat and lifeless. This use of imagination must be judicious, however. Readers must be careful to distinguish between what the text strongly suggests, what it permits, and what is pure speculation. In any case, only what the text says can claim scriptural authority.

Finally, and above all else, one must read the Bible. Evidence suggests that, nowadays, even believers read the Bible less than previous generations. People often report that the Bible seems foreign or difficult to understand. As they understand less, they are prone to read less; as they read less, they understand less. The system feeds on itself. Recognizing and appreciating the humor in the Bible is but one avenue toward bringing the Bible back to vital and vibrant prominence in the lives of modern believers. The urgent need is for a community of believers who spend time with Scripture—exploring it, contemplating it, and seeking to enter into its broad, profound, sometimes incongruous world.

Note

1. The Hebrew term *elohim* is ambiguous. By form a plural, in various contexts it can refer to the one God of Israel, the gods of the nations, or angelic beings. In the context of Ps 8, the precise connotation of the term is unclear.

For Further Reading

Adams, D. *The Prostitute in the Family Tree: Discovering Humor and Irony in the Bible*. Louisville KY: Westminster/JKP, 1997.

Arbuckle, G. A. *Laughing with God: Humor, Culture, and Transformation*. Collegeville MN: Liturgical Press, 2008.

Berger, P. *Redeeming Laughter: The Comic Dimension of Human Experience*. Berlin: de Gruyter, 1997.

Comier, H. *The Humor of Jesus*. New York: Alban House, 1977.

Corrigan, R. W., editor. *Comedy: Meaning and Form*. Scranton PA: Chandler Publishing Co., 1965.

Darden, R. *Jesus Laughed: The Redemptive Power of Humor*. Nashville: Abingdon, 2008.

Eastman, M., editor. *Enjoyment of Laughter*. New York: Simon and Schuster, 1936.

Fisher, S., et al. *Pretend the World Is Funny and Forever: A Psychological Analysis of Comedians, Clowns and Actors*. Hillsdale NJ: Laurence Erlbaum, 1981.

Fuchs, E. "Laughing With/At/As Women," in A. Brenner, editor, *Are We Amused? Humour about Women in the Biblical Worlds*. JSOTS 383; Bible in the Twenty-First Century Series 2. New York: T & T Clark, 2003.

Gaddy, C. W. *God's Clowns: Messengers of the Good News*. San Francisco: Harper & Row, 1990.

Good, E. M. *Irony in the Old Testament*. Philadelphia: Westminster, 1965.

Gruner, C. R. *Understanding Laughter*. Chicago: Nelson-Hal, 1978.

Hyers, M. C., editor. *Holy Laughter: Essays on Religion in the Comic Perspective*. New York: The Seabury Press, 1969.

―――. *The Comic Vision and the Christian Faith: A Celebration of Life and Laughter*. New York: Pilgrim Press, 1981.

―――. *And God Created Laughter: The Bible as Divine Comedy*. Atlanta: John Knox Press, 1987.

Jackson, M. "Lot's Daughters and Tamar as Tricksters and the Patriarchal Narratives as Feminist Theology." *JSOT* 98 (2002): 29–46.

Jameson, J. "Humour and Other Features of the Style of Jesus," in *Why Jesus Died*. Glasgow: Strickland, 1948.

Jemielity, T. *Satire and the Hebrew Prophets*. Literary Currents in Biblical Interpretation. Louisville: Westminster/John Knox, 1992.

Johnson, E. *A Treasury of Satire: The Nature and Volume of Satire*. New York: Simon and Schuster, 1945.

Jónsson, J. *Humour and Irony in the New Testament*. Beihefte der Zeitschrift für Religions und Geistesgeschichte 28. Leiden: Brill, 1985.

Kantra, R. A. *All Things Vain: Religious Satirists and Their Art*. University Park PA: The Pennsylvania State University Press, 1984.

Kuschel, Karl-Josef. *Laughter: A Theological Essay*. New York: Continuum, 1994.

Levine, A.-J. "Women, Humor and Other Creative Juices," in Brenner, editor, *Are We Amused?*

Levine, N. "'Twice as Much of Your Spirit': Pattern, Parallel and Paronomasia in the Miracles of Elijah and Elisha." *JSOT* 85 (1999): 85–46.

Marcus, D. *From Balaam to Jonah: Anti-Prophetic Satire in the Hebrew Bible*. Atlanta: Scholars Press, 1995.

Mikes, G. *Laughing Matters: Toward a Personal Philosophy of Wit and Humor*. New York: Library Press, 1971.

Morreall, J. *Comedy, Tragedy, and Religion*. Albany: SUNY Press, 1999.

———. *Taking Laughter Seriously*. Albany: SUNY Press, 1983.

Niditch, S., editor. *Text and Tradition: The Hebrew Bible and Folklore*. Atlanta: Scholars Press, 1990.

O'Connor, K. M. "Humor, Turnabouts and Survival in the Book of Esther," in Brenner, editor, *Are We Amused?*

Parrott, B. W. *God's Sense of Humor*. New York: Philosophical Library, 1984.

———. *Ontology of Humor*. New York: Philosophical Library, 1982.

Phipps, W. E. *The Wisdom and Wit of Rabbi Jesus*. Louisville: Westminster/John Knox, 1983.

Radday, Y. T., and A. Brenner, editors. *On Humour and the Comic in the Hebrew Bible*. Sheffield: Almond, 1990.

Shields, M. E. "More Righteous Than I," in Brenner, editor, *Are We Amused?*

Spencer, F. S. "Those Riotous—Yet Righteous—Foremothers of Jesus," in Brenner, editor, *Are We Amused?*

Trueblood, E. *The Humor of Christ.* New York: Harper & Row, 1964.

Vos, N. *For God's Sake Laugh!* Richmond: John Knox, 1967.

Whedbee, J. W. *The Bible and the Comic Vision.* New York: Cambridge University Press, 1998.

Williams, K. C. "At the Expense of Women," in Brenner, editor, *Are We Amused?*

Other available titles from

Daniel (Smyth & Helwys Annual Bible Study series)
Keeping Faith When the Heat Is On
Bill Ireland

Daniel is a book about resistance. It was written to people under
pressure. In the book, we will see the efforts oppressive regimes
take to undermine the faith and identity of God's people. In it, we
will also see the strategies God's people employed in resisting the imposition of a
foreign culture, and we will see what sustained their efforts. In that vein, the book
of Daniel is powerfully relevant.   *Teaching Guide 978-1-57312-647-2 144 pages/pb* **$14.00**

Study Guide 978-1-57312-646-5 80 pages/pb **$6.00**

A Divine Duet
Ministry and Motherhood
Alicia Davis Porterfield, ed.

Each essay in this inspiring collection is as different as the mother-
minister who wrote it, from theologians to chaplains, inner-city
ministers to rural-poverty ministers, youth pastors to preachers,
mothers who have adopted, birthed, and done both.

978-1-57312-676-2 146 pages/pb **$16.00**

Divorce Ministry
A Guidebook
Charles Qualls

This book shares with the reader the value of establishing a divorce
recovery ministry while also offering practical insights on establishing your own unique church-affiliated program. Whether you
are working individually with one divorced person or leading a large group, *Divorce
Ministry: A Guidebook* provides helpful resources to guide you through the emo-
tional and relational issues divorced people often encounter.

978-1-57312-588-8 156 pages/pb **$16.00**

The Enoch Factor
The Sacred Art of Knowing God
Steve McSwain

The Enoch Factor is a persuasive argument for a more enlightened
religious dialogue in America, one that affirms the goals of all
religions—guiding followers in self-awareness, finding serenity and
happiness, and discovering what the author describes as "the sacred art of knowing
God."   *978-1-57312-556-7 256 pages/pb* **$21.00**

To order call 1-800-747-3016 or visit www.helwys.com

Healing Our Hurts
Coping with Difficult Emotions
Daniel Bagby

In *Healing Our Hurts*, Daniel Bagby identifies and explains all the dynamics at play in these complex emotions. Offering practical biblical insights to these feelings, he interprets faith-based responses to separate overly religious piety from true, natural human emotion. This book helps us learn how to deal with life's difficult emotions in a redemptive and responsible way. *978-1-57312-613-7 144 pages/pb* **$15.00**

Hope for the Thinking Christian
Seeking a Path of Faith through Everyday Life
Stephen Reese

Readers who want to confront their faith more directly, to think it through and be open to God in an individual, authentic, spiritual encounter will find a resonant voice in Stephen Reese.

978-1-57312-553-6 160 pages/pb **$16.00**

A Hungry Soul Desperate to Taste God's Grace
Honest Prayers for Life
Charles Qualls

Part of how we *see* God is determined by how we *listen* to God. There is so much noise and movement in the world that competes with images of God. This noise would drown out God's beckoning voice and distract us. Charles Qualls's newest book offers readers prayers for that journey toward the meaning and mystery of God. *978-1-57312-648-9 152 pages/pb* **$14.00**

James M. Dunn and Soul Freedom
Aaron Douglas Weaver

James Milton Dunn, over the last fifty years, has been the most aggressive Baptist proponent for religious liberty in the United States. Soul freedom—voluntary, uncoerced faith and an unfettered individual conscience before God—is the basis of his understanding of church-state separation and the historic Baptist basis of religious liberty.

978-1-57312-590-1 224 pages/pb **$18.00**

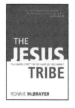

The Jesus Tribe
Following Christ in the Land of the Empire
Ronnie McBrayer

The Jesus Tribe fleshes out the implications, possibilities, contradictions, and complexities of what it means to live within the Jesus Tribe and in the shadow of the American Empire.

978-1-57312-592-5 208 pages/pb **$17.00**

Judaism
A Brief Guide to Faith and Practice
Sharon Pace

Sharon Pace's newest book is a sensitive and comprehensive introduction to Judaism. What is it like to be born into the Jewish community? How does belief in the One God and a universal morality shape the way in which Jews see the world? How does one find meaning in life and the courage to endure suffering? How does one mark joy and forge community ties? *978-1-57312-644-1 144 pages/pb* **$16.00**

Lessons from the Cloth 2
501 More One Minute Motivators for Leaders
Bo Prosser and Charles Qualls

As the force that drives organizations to accomplishment, leadership is at a crucial point in churches, corporations, families, and almost every arena of life. Without leadership there is chaos. *With* leadership there is sometimes chaos! In this follow-up to their first volume, Bo Prosser and Charles Qualls will inspire you to keep growing in your leadership career. *978-1-57312-665-6 152 pages/pb* **$11.00**

Let Me More of Their Beauty See
Reading Familiar Verses in Context
Diane G. Chen

Let Me More of Their Beauty See offers eight examples of how attention to the historical and literary settings can safeguard against taking a text out of context, bring out its transforming power in greater dimension, and help us apply Scripture appropriately in our daily lives. *978-1-57312-564-2 160 pages/pb* **$17.00**

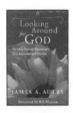

Looking Around for God
The Strangely Reverent Observations of an Unconventional Christian
James A. Autry

Looking Around for God, Autry's tenth book, is in many ways his most personal. In it he considers his unique life of faith and belief in God. Autry is a former Fortune 500 executive, author, poet, and consultant whose work has had a significant influence on leadership thinking.

978-157312-484-3 144 pages/pb **$16.00**

Maggie Lee for Good

Jinny and John Hinson

Maggie Lee for Good captures the essence of a young girl's boundless faith and spirit. Her parents' moving story of the accident that took her life will inspire readers who are facing loss, looking for evidence of God's sustaining grace, or searching for ways to make a meaningful difference in the lives of others. *978-1-57312-630-4 144 pages/pb* **$15.00**

Making the Timeless Word Timely

A Primer for Preachers

Michael B. Brown

Michael Brown writes, "There is a simple formula for sermon preparation that creates messages that apply and engage whether your parish is rural or urban, young or old, rich or poor, five thousand members or fifty." The other part of the task, of course, involves being creative and insightful enough to know how to take the general formula for sermon preparation and make it particular in its impact on a specific congregation. Brown guides the reader through the formula and the skills to employ it with excellence and integrity. *978-1-57312-578-9 160 pages/pb* **$16.00**

Meeting Jesus Today

For the Cautious, the Curious, and the Committed

Jeanie Miley

Meeting Jesus Today, ideal for both individual study and small groups, is intended to be used as a workbook. It is designed to move readers from studying the Scriptures and ideas within the chapters to recording their journey with the Living Christ.

978-1-57312-677-9 320 pages/pb **$19.00**

The Ministry Life

101 Tips for New Ministers

John Killinger

Sharing years of wisdom from more than fifty years in ministry and teaching, *The Ministry Life: 101 Tips for New Ministers* by John Killinger is filled with practical advice and wisdom for a minister's day-to-day tasks as well as advice on intellectual and spiritual habits to keep ministers of any age healthy and fulfilled. *978-1-57312-662-5 244 pages/pb* **$19.00**

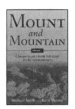

Mount and Mountain
Vol. 1: A Reverend and a Rabbi Talk About the Ten Commandments

Rami Shapiro and Michael Smith

Mount and Mountain represents the first half of an interfaith dialogue—a dialogue that neither preaches nor placates but challenges its participants to work both singly and together in the task of reinterpreting sacred texts. Mike and Rami discuss the nature of divinity, the power of faith, the beauty of myth and story, the necessity of doubt, the achievements, failings, and future of religion, and, above all, the struggle to live ethically and in harmony with the way of God.　　*978-1-57312-612-0 144 pages/pb* **$15.00**

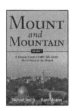

Mount and Mountain
Vol. 2: A Reverend and a Rabbi Talk About the Sermon on the Mount

Rami Shapiro and Michael Smith

This book, focused on the Sermon on the Mount, represents the second half of Mike and Rami's dialogue. In it, Mike and Rami explore the text of Jesus' sermon cooperatively, contributing perspectives drawn from their lives and religious traditions and seeking moments of illumination.　　*978-1-57312-654-0 254 pages/pb* **$19.00**

Overcoming Adolescence
Growing Beyond Childhood into Maturity

Marion D. Aldridge

In *Overcoming Adolescence*, Marion Aldridge poses questions for adults of all ages to consider. His challenge to readers is one he has personally worked to confront: to grow up *all the way*—mentally, physically, academically, socially, emotionally, and spiritually. The key involves not only knowing how to work through the process but also how to recognize what may be contributing to our perpetual adolescence.

978-1-57312-577-2 156 pages/pb **$17.00**

Psychic Pancakes & Communion Pizza
More Musings and Mutterings of a Church Misfit

Bert Montgomery

Psychic Pancakes & Communion Pizza is Bert Montgomery's highly anticipated follow-up to *Elvis, Willie, Jesus & Me* and contains further reflections on music, film, culture, life, and finding Jesus in the midst of it all.　　*978-1-57312-578-9 160 pages/pb* **$16.00**

Quiet Faith
An Introvert's Guide to Spiritual Survival
Judson Edwards

In eight finely crafted chapters, Edwards look at key issues like evangelism, interpreting the Bible, dealing with doubt, and surviving the church from the perspective of a confirmed, but sometimes reluctant, introvert. In the process, he offers some provocative insights that introverts will find helpful and reassuring. *978-1-57312-681-6 144 pages/pb* **$15.00**

Reading Ezekiel (Reading the Old Testament series)
A Literary and Theological Commentary
Marvin A. Sweeney

The book of Ezekiel points to the return of YHWH to the holy temple at the center of a reconstituted Israel and creation at large. As such, the book of Ezekiel portrays the purging of Jerusalem, the Temple, and the people, to reconstitute them as part of a new creation at the conclusion of the book. With Jerusalem, the Temple, and the people so purged, YHWH stands once again in the holy center of the created world.

978-1-57312-658-8 264 pages/pb **$22.00**

Reading Job (Reading the Old Testament series)
A Literary and Theological Commentary
James L. Crenshaw

At issue in the Book of Job is a question with which most all of us struggle at some point in life, "Why do bad things happen to good people?" James Crenshaw has devoted his life to studying the disturbing matter of theodicy—divine justice—that troubles many people of faith.

978-1-57312-574-1 192 pages/pb **$22.00**

Reading Judges (Reading the Old Testament series)
A Literary and Theological Commentary
Mark E. Biddle

Reading the Old Testament book of Judges presents a number of significant challenges related to social contexts, historical settings, and literary characteristics. Acknowledging and examining these difficulties provides a point of entry into the world of Judges and promises to enrich the reading experience. *978-1-57312-631-1 240 pages/pb* **$22.00**

Reading Samuel (Reading the Old Testament series)
A Literary and Theological Commentary
Johanna W. H. van Wijk-Bos

Interpreted masterfully by preeminent Old Testament scholar Johanna W. H. van Wijk-Bos, the story of Samuel touches on a vast array of subjects that make up the rich fabric of human life. The reader gains an inside look at leadership, royal intrigue, military campaigns, occult practices, and the significance of religious objects of veneration.

978-1-57312-607-6 272 pages/pb **$22.00**

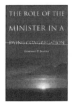

The Role of the Minister in a Dying Congregation
Lynwood B. Jenkins

Jenkins provides a courageous and responsible resource on one of the most critical issues in congregational life: how to help a congregation conclude its ministry life cycle with dignity and meaning.

978-1-57312-571-0 96 pages/pb **$14.00**

Sessions with Genesis (Session Bible Studies series)
The Story Begins
Tony W. Cartledge

Immersing us in the book of Genesis, Tony Cartledge examines both its major stories and the smaller cycles of hope and failure, of promise and judgment. Genesis introduces these themes of divine faithfulness and human failure in unmistakable terms, tracing Israel's beginning to the creation of the world and professing a belief that Israel's particular history had universal significance. *978-1-57312-636-6 144 pages/pb* **$14.00**

Sessions with Philippians (Session Bible Studies series)
Finding Joy in Community
Bo Prosser

In this brief letter to the Philippians, Paul makes clear the centrality of his faith in Jesus Christ, his love for the Philippian church, and his joy in serving both Christ and their church.

978-1-57312-579-6 112 pages/pb **$13.00**

Sessions with Samuel (Session Bible Studies series)
Stories from the Edge
Tony W. Cartledge

In these stories, Israel faces one crisis after another, a people constantly on the edge. Individuals such as Saul and David find themselves on the edge as well, facing troubles of leadership and personal struggle. Yet, each crisis becomes a gateway for learning that God is always present, that hope remains. *978-1-57312-555-0 112 pages/pb* **$13.00**

Silver Linings
My Life Before and After Challenger 7
June Scobee Rodgers

We know the public story of *Challenger 7*'s tragic destruction. That day, June's life took a new direction that ultimately led to the creation of the Challenger Center and to new life and new love. Her story of Christian faith and triumph over adversity will inspire readers of every age.
978-1-57312-570-3 *352 pages/hc* **$28.00**

Spacious
Exploring Faith and Place
Holly Sprink

Exploring where we are and why that matters to God is an ongoing process. If we are present and attentive, God creatively and continuously widens our view of the world, whether we live in the Amazon or in our own hometown. 978-1-57312-649-6 *156 pages/pb* **$16.00**

This Is What a Preacher Looks Like
Sermons by Baptist Women in Ministry
Pamela Durso, ed.

In this collection of sermons by thirty-six Baptist women, their voices are soft and loud, prophetic and pastoral, humorous and sincere. They are African American, Asian, Latina, and Caucasian. They are sisters, wives, mothers, grandmothers, aunts, and friends.
978-1-57312-554-3 *144 pages/pb* **$18.00**

Transformational Leadership
Leading with Integrity
Charles B. Bugg

"Transformational" leadership involves understanding and growing so that we can help create positive change in the world. This book encourages leaders to be willing to change if *they* want to help transform the world. They are honest about their personal strengths and weaknesses, and are not afraid of doing a fearless moral inventory of themselves.
978-1-57312-558-1 *112 pages/pb* **$14.00**

Made in the USA
Middletown, DE
30 October 2014